THE ART OF THE ARTISTIC DIRECTOR

- research Hope history
- research Islington community to be served
- partners: Global origins, LIVR, other theatre co's?
- develop projects?
- producing models – resources v projects tradeoff (quantity/quality)

- look at accounts of charity for more detail
- p6 trying to address middle class structures
- try + curate seasons or at least ~~mini~~-seasons?
- worth talking about ~~loosen~~ loosening current tight/specific rules/structures – find some room for controlled flexibility?
- new talent, the overlooked, discovery, providing 'hope'

THE ART OF THE ARTISTIC DIRECTOR

Conversations with Leading Practitioners

CHRISTOPHER HAYDON

methuen | drama
LONDON • NEW YORK • OXFORD • NEW DELHI • SYDNEY

METHUEN DRAMA
Bloomsbury Publishing Plc
50 Bedford Square, London, WC1B 3DP, UK
1385 Broadway, New York, NY 10018, USA

BLOOMSBURY, METHUEN DRAMA and the Methuen Drama
logo are trademarks of Bloomsbury Publishing Plc

First published in Great Britain 2019
Reprinted 2019

Cover design by Daniel Benneworth-Gray

A catalogue record for this book is available from the British Library.

Library of Congress Cataloging-in-Publication Data
Names: Haydon, Christopher, author.
Title: Art of the artistic director : conversations with leading practitioners / Christopher Haydon.
Description: London, UK ; New York, NY : Methuen Drama, 2019.
Identifiers: LCCN 2018035499| ISBN 9781350016927 (hb) | ISBN 9781350016934 (pb) | ISBN 9781350016941 (ePUB) | ISBN 9781350016958 (ePDF)
Subjects: LCSH: Theater–Production and direction–Interviews. | Theatrical producers and directors–Interviews.
Classification: LCC PN2053 .H338 2019 | DDC 792.02/32–dc23 LC record available at https://lccn.loc.gov/2018035499

ISBN: HB: 978-1-3500-1692-7
PB: 978-1-3500-1693-4
ePDF: 978-1-3500-1695-8
eBook: 978-1-3500-1694-1

Typeset by Integra Software Services Pvt. Ltd.
Printed and bound in Great Britain

In memory of Crispian Pickles and Anne Carroll. Who both inspired in me a deep love of theatre as a teenager. May they rest in peace.

And to Lynette Linton, who is going to do *magnificent* things at the Bush Theatre.

CONTENTS

FOREWORD

MICHAEL GRANDAGE

I welcome a book on the role of the artistic director. It is a little discussed, highly nuanced job that requires a very particular skill, and Christopher Haydon offers a fascinating series of interviews that allow us into the minds of those who have put themselves forward to develop the life of an organization in full public view.

Whether it's developing a house style under one roof for those who have buildings or integrating into the fabric of a community for those who don't, it requires a very specific focus that has less to do with being a director and far more to do with being a creative producer.

With a few honourable exceptions, there is a constant turnover of artistic directors in the UK. The model is very different in New York City where the permanence of an artistic director is seen as a mark of stability. The common link between both is the tenacious ambition a good artistic director has for their organization. It rises above the personal and these illuminating interviews give us a glimpse of who is best placed for this most peculiar job.

Michael Grandage was artistic director of Sheffield Crucible from 1999 to 2005 and of the Donmar Warehouse in London from 2002 to 2012.

ACKNOWLEDGEMENTS

As will become clear in the following pages, no artistic director can thrive without the support of a whole array of remarkable collaborators. I would not have been able to write this book if it hadn't been for what I learned from the exceptional friendships and creative partnerships that I formed while I was running the Gate Theatre. Chief among all of these was my collaboration with Clare Slater, my executive director for most of my time running the theatre. She was my partner in crime, and the key brain behind all of our successes; she is one of the finest people in the British theatre industry. I am also, inevitably, massively indebted to my partner in life, Iona Firouzabadi. She is a fine artist in her own right, my greatest supporter and my most acerbic critic.

I am hugely grateful to all those who took time out of their insanely busy schedules to be interviewed for this book. And I am very thankful to the Clore Leadership Programme and the Gatsby Charitable Trust, without whose support I would not have been able to carry out this research.

Mentorship is a vital part of an artistic director's job, and I have been lucky to get guidance from some exceptional people in this regard. In particular I would like to thank: Michael Boyd, Mick Gordon, Michael Grandage, David Lan, Tom Morris, Josie Rourke, Philip Wilson and Erica Whyman.

Finally, I tip my hat to all of those exceptional individuals and artists who have challenged and inspired me in my capacity as an artistic director and as a freelance theatre maker. Any successes I had at the Gate are entirely down to them: Hassan Abdulrazzak, Natalie Abrahami, Stefan Adegbola, Marcus Adolphy, Michael Ajao, Akala, Sian Alexander, Teresa Alpert, Chrissy Angus, Sharon Armstrong-Williams, Lily Arnold, Justin Audibert, Alex Baranowski, Chris Barter, Katrina Barter, Mark Bayley,

Shakti Bhagchandani, Oliver Birch, Caroline Bird, Jeremy Blocker, Dave Bond, Adam Brace, Jack Bradfield, Frankie Bradshaw, George Brant, Michael Brazier, Louise Brealey, Liam Brennan, Neil Brener, Sarah Brener, Howard Brenton, Andrea Brooks, Alex Brown, Lucy Brown, Natasha Brown, Susan Brown, Fumilayo Brown-Olateju, Natasha Bucknor, Nica Burns, Daniel Bye, Caroline Byrne, Lorne Campbell, Silas Carson, Sarah Chappatte, Rachel Chavkin, Lois Chimimba, Jude Christian, Chipo Chung, Lauren Clancy, Guy Clarke, Ed Collier, Elinor Cook, Daisy Cooper, Charles Cormick, Carrie Cracknell, Linda Crooks, James Dacre, Josie Dale-Jones, Becky Darlington, Arthur Darvill, Fly Davis, Fay Davies, Kate Denby, George Dennis, Robert Devereux, Pip Donaghy, Heather Doole, Amy Draper, Noma Dumezweni, Ari Edelson, David Edgar, Lily Einhorn, Suhayla El-Bushra, Lucy Ellinson, Chloe Elwood, Sue Emmas, Fiona English, Katy Munroe Farlie, Andy Field, Polly Findlay, Sally Fleming, Jon Foster, Polly Frame, Chloe France, Liz Frankel, Ed Franklin, William Gaminara, Lyn Gardner, Lilli Geissendorfer, Di Glazer, Rupert Goold, Jan Grandison, Richard Grandison, Eloise Green, Adam Greenfield, Tamsin Greig, Colin Grenfell, Danai Gurira, Yasmin Hafesji, Jenny Hall, Johann Hari, Brian Hastert, Robert Hewison, Rebecca Hill, Anna Himali-Howard, Lucas Hnath, Kobna Holdbrook-Smith, Bethany Holmes, Sean Holmes, Suli Holum, Bernard Horn, Clare Horn, Juliette Howell, Mark Howland, Sue Hoyle, Jonathan Hull, Nick Hytner, Maya Ingram, Elayce Ismail, Joan Iyiola, Gabriella Jeffries, Melanie Jessop, Priya Jethwa, Sholeh Joseph, Aditi Kapil, Bobette Kenge, Bill Kenwright, Paul Keogan, Ben Kidd, Terry King, Jonathan Kinnersley, Euan Kitson, Wendy Kweh, David Lakhdir, Linda Lakhdir, Rita Laven, Jade Lewis, Emily Lim, Lynette Linton, Ethan Lipton, Tom Littler, Jonathan Lomma, Suzann MacLean, Annie MacRae, Ed Madden, Raphael Martin, Ellen McDougall, Louise McMenemy, Jeremy Meadow, Hattie Morahan, Purni Morell, Kate Morley, Elisabeth Morse, Lucian Msamati, David Muse, Mimi Ndiweni, Nicole Newman, Lindsay Nock, Barney Norris, Bruce Norris, Kady Howey Nunn, Dan O'Brien, Kate O'Connor, John O'Donovan, Chinonyerem Odimba, Orla O'Loughlin, Anastasia Osei-Kuffour, Emilie Patry, Deborah Pearson, Elena Pena, Richard Pepple, Clare Perkins, Danielle Phillips, Ali Pidsley, Holly Piggot, Anna Poole, Barbara Prideaux, Charles Prideaux , Sarah Punshon, Lulu Raczka, Adam Rapp, Matilda Reith, William Reynolds, Mark Robinson, Tessa Ross, Jo Royce, Suzy Sancho, Anne-Louise Sarks, Andrew Schneider, Jon Sedmak, NoraLee Sedmak, Nina Segal, Nitzan

Sharron, Raz Shaw, Giles Smart, Al Smith, Joseph Smith, Aaron Sorkin, Jason Southgate, Kalungi Ssebandeke, Nick Starr, Deborah Stein, Mark Subias, Alex Swift, Jennifer Tang, Shannon Tarbet, Nicola Maisie Taylor, Kate Thorogood, Chris Thorpe, Monique Touko, Oli Townsend, Lyndsey Turner, Petia Tzanova, Bea Udale-Smith, Jake Ulrich, Sandi Ulrich, Anjana Vasan, Rachel Viola, Ella Wahlström, Imogen Walford, Eileen Walsh, Paul Warwick, Kate Wasserberg, Charlotte Westenra, Donato Wharton, Steve Wheeler, James Wilkinson, Matthew Wilkinson, Rachael Williams, Letitia Wright and Ashley Zhangazha.

My profuse apologies to anyone whom I have inadvertently left out.

A NOTE ON THE SPELLING OF THE WORD 'THEATRE' (OR, ER, 'THEATER')

Americans spell the word 'theatre' differently to Brits – they prefer to reverse the final two letters making it 'theater'. They don't actually seem entirely convinced by this spelling however, and so while some US venues use it (e.g. The Public Theater), others choose the UK version (e.g. Goodman Theatre). In this book I stick with the British spelling of the word whenever it is used in conversation except where it appears as part of the name of a venue in which case I spell it in whichever way the institution itself uses. For an artform that thrives on the complexities, ambiguities and contradictions of language, this confusion feels sort of appropriate.

INTRODUCTION

In mid-2011, I received a phone call to offer me the job of artistic director at the Gate Theatre in London. Having realized, through the intensive interview process, quite how much I wanted the gig, my instinctive response was, unsurprisingly, one of elation. I accepted on the spot. But almost as soon as I had hung up the phone, the adrenaline rush gave way to something else – abject fear. What the hell was I doing? I'd never run a business in my life. Sure, the Gate was quite a small theatre, but it had an extraordinary history and was a vital part of the UK theatre ecology. What if I bankrupted the place?

I decided I needed help pretty urgently. So I got in touch with Erica Whyman who had become something of a mentor to me. At the time she was artistic director of Northern Stage in Newcastle and, crucially, she had run the Gate some years before. I bought her a coffee and explained my fear that my tenure might be terminal for the venue. Almost before I had finished speaking, she looked me in the eye and said: 'Oh, don't be so ridiculous. You're not going to bankrupt the Gate!' Erica has always had a reassuring manner, and while I can't now remember exactly what her argument was, those words would come back to me in the following years whenever I worried about whether or not to take a particular risk.

As I settled into the job I was fortunate to be offered guidance by another remarkable artistic director: David Lan of the Young Vic. We met when I was in the middle of planning my first season. I told him that I felt like I was on an incredibly steep learning curve. He smiled and said that it would never get any less steep. It was curiously reassuring to feel that even someone as experienced as him felt like they were still trying to figure everything out. The problem was not me; rather, there just wasn't really a road map for a job like this. Every venue is different and an artistic director has to be led by their own personal passions –

so running a venue is as unique a process as writing a novel, painting a picture or, well, directing a play.

By the time I left the Gate in early 2017, I had reached a point where I honestly didn't know where I ended and the Gate began. It had been an all-consuming experience. Exhilarating and terrifying in equal measure, it has, without doubt, been the best five years of my life so far. But I also felt acutely aware that for many people, the job I had been doing seemed quite mysterious. For instance, I was asked, on more than one occasion: 'Who gets to pick the plays in the theatre you run?' I was often greeted with a look of surprise when I said that that was precisely what my job was all about.

This incomprehension around what an artistic director does is, perhaps, not a surprise. Despite the fact that they are among the most powerful people in the theatre industry, there is almost nothing written about the job they do. There are a small handful of excellent books: *Free for All* by Joseph Papp and Kenneth Turan gives a vital portrait of the inner workings of The Public Theater in New York in its early years, Peter Hall and Richard Eyre both wrote compelling diaries about their tenures at the National Theatre (NT), and most recently Nick Hytner's *Balancing Acts* gives his own account of running the NT. But beyond those, which focus only on the largest institutions, there is very little else.

It would have been an act of spectacular hubris to think that my time at a tiny venue like the Gate would qualify me to write a book on how to run a theatre. But, I thought, maybe that experience at least meant that I'd be able to ask the right questions of those who'd been doing it for much longer than me. And perhaps, by creating space for my colleagues to share their experiences in their own words, I would be able to give others an insight into this peculiar job.

I decided to focus, for the most part, on people who run actual theatre buildings (rather than non-building-based touring companies). Partly this is because that is where my own experience lies. But also, it is because I have a profound belief in the value of bricks and mortar. There are, of course, many exceptional companies that don't have their own home. But a theatre building has both the capacity and the responsibility to be a permanent focal point for a community. At its best, it can act like a secular church: a place where people can congregate regularly to explore what it means to be human. For similar reasons I chose to focus on those venues that are either not-for-profits (as they are termed in the United States) or charities in receipt of public subsidy (as they are in the UK). These venues are often the ones able to take the boldest artistic risks, which they must then combine with an obligation to serve the public good. As such, the people running them must be particularly visionary and ambitious in their work.

As for my decision to focus specifically on venues in the UK and the United States? Well, just as when I ran my own theatre, that decision comes down essentially to my own particular artistic tastes. I've always been fascinated by the United States, and I chose to programme many American plays at the Gate. And as with so many things when it comes to comparing our two countries, our respective theatre cultures are very similar in some ways and profoundly different in others. But at a time when both the UK and the United States are going through periods of seismic political instability – caused by Brexit and Trump, respectively – it feels particularly valuable to see what we might be able to learn from each other.

Inevitably, there are numerous exceptional artistic directors for whom I did not have space to include here. Many of those are name-checked in these pages by the people I did speak to. One of the most inspiring things about working in the theatre is that, as an industry, it really does produce exceptional leaders. Very few people enter this profession with the belief that they will earn their fortunes through it. They do it because they love it; because they can't *not* do it. Perhaps that is why they are so good at it.

1
SARAH BENSON

Sarah Benson has been artistic director of Soho Rep since 2007. Soho Rep is a small studio theatre in Lower Manhattan dedicated to producing innovative contemporary theatre.

Could you tell me about your journey to running Soho Rep?
I'm from Southampton in the UK originally. I'd been making work in London when I was offered a Fulbright Scholarship to do an MFA in Directing at Brooklyn College. My husband and I came over to New York so I could do that, but we planned to move right back to London afterwards. I did the MFA for two years, which was fantastic, and then there was the option of a third year under the auspices of Fulbright. Several people who I knew, both in New York and the UK, kept saying to me: 'You should check out this theatre Soho Rep. It's really up your street.' So I came and saw the work and loved it. I then interviewed for an internship with Young Jean Lee who at that time worked here and I remember her saying 'Don't take the internship!' But I ended up taking it mainly because I had loved the production of Maria Irene Fornes's *Molly's Dream* so much and I wanted to find out how that got made. So I interned for a year under my predecessor Daniel Aukin. One of the programmes that Soho Rep runs is the Writer/Director Lab – where writers and directors develop projects from the ground up. Daniel asked me to take over co-chairing it, and that was a great chance to just jump into something.

At the same time I had a conversation with Frank Hentschker at the Segal Theater Center which is part of CUNY.[1] This is an amazing place that works to bridge the professional and academic worlds. They had

[1] City University of New York.

this festival called Prelude, but Frank was ready to throw in the towel with it. So I told him that I'd like to take a shot at curating it for a year, which he allowed me to do. So between the Lab and Prelude I had this incredible opportunity to start picking up the phone and calling artists.

That was the beginning of things. Up until then I had only seen myself as a director. But the experience of working on those projects made me realize that I really enjoy the process of curating and of being surrounded by people whose processes are so different from mine. Being challenged by that was very inspiring. And having been an outsider to the New York theatre scene, I suddenly found myself completely welcomed by this community.

The year after that, Daniel decided he wanted to go freelance and he resigned. At the time, my husband and I were trying to decide whether to stay in New York or move back to Europe. And I applied really not thinking that I would have a chance. I thought they would hire someone who really knew how to run a theatre and had done it before. And so I was surprised when the board offered me the position. And now I have been here ten years!

How conscious did you feel of Soho Rep's history when you took over? Do you feel that it shaped you? And how much do you think you have had the ability to shape it in return?

The history of the theatre goes back to when Marlene Swartz and Jerry Engelbach founded it in the 1970s. At that point they were doing ten shows a year for a total cost of around $90,000 – which feels incredible and crazy now! They were doing a lot of neglected classics, but I think the throughline was about engaging with language and how language functions in the theatre. When Daniel took over, he focused on new work exclusively. Everything we do now is new. Either it's a commission or it's something that we have found or developed from the ground up. Very occasionally we will produce the US or New York premiere of a new international play, like we did with debbie tucker green's plays *born bad* and *generations* or Alice Birch's *Revolt She Said, Revolt Again.*

Daniel also began to shift the producing model. Previously, it had been about giving a lot of people opportunities – being this hot bed for artists to try stuff. But he shifted it to be about putting more significant resources behind fewer projects – with the aim that we should be creating the very best versions of the work that we possibly could. That's something I really believe in and have continued to develop. Soho Rep is one of the few places that will give a really full-throated production to an unconventional artist who has maybe never had a show before. Many of the larger off-Broadway theatres are just not in a place where they are able to do that for someone who is completely unproduced.

It's also been important to me to address our history as a predominantly white institution and ask how we can be an anti-racist theatre. There is such deep structural bias in the field, especially in 'experimental theatre' that basically exists outside any meaningful economic system. It inherently privileges people who have the cultural capital to work for close to free. That creates a lot of white work. And that work in turn dominates the conversation as those are the artists who have had the opportunities to develop their voices early on and who are later deemed 'off-Broadway ready'. It is an impoverished conversation and one that of course only feeds and perpetuates the oppressive structures. So that is something we are constantly trying to work against and transform.

How does your programming process work? What draws you to a particular project and how do you go about curating a specific season?

This season is a good example of how we programme in terms of process, as the projects have had such radically different paths to production. Aleshea Harris's play *Is God Is* was sent to me by Branden Jacobs-Jenkins. I read it one night and emailed Aleshea the next morning to talk about doing the play. The text was brilliant and indestructible and barely changed during our process. Jackie Sibblies Drury's play *Fairview* alternately began three years ago as a co-commission with Berkeley Rep. It has come through our development programming at the theatre over a two-year period and has taken on many different forms as Jackie has generated this incredibly exciting text through a workshop process.

We approach every project we are doing differently: whether it's playwright driven or more director driven. We've even done some design-driven projects. We worked with Louisa Thompson who instigated and designed a project called *Washeteria* that was set site-specifically in a Laundromat. At the first rehearsal, we didn't have a script, we just had a design model and the writers César Alvarez and Charise Castro Smith responded to that. And when we did Sarah Kane's *Blasted*, that was instigated by the actor Marin Ireland. The urgency she felt to do the play at that time was infectious.

Sometimes it feels as if we are reinventing the company in response to how each particular project needs to be produced. So we don't have specific 'slots' or a particular protocol for how we produce. It's driven by the needs of the project and the particular alchemy of people who have gathered to do it. And while text is very much a throughline in our work, I'm super interested in giving directors space to instigate things.

I guess I'm mostly interested in artists who have a destabilizing force. That will often start from me reading something or seeing something that I'm challenged by or that makes me feel uncomfortable or embarrassed. I find that those are very fruitful feelings to dig in to.

Do you seek to develop longer-term relationships with artists? Or does it tend to be more on a project-by-project basis?

I feel like part of our role in the landscape is to shine a light on the brand new or the overlooked. So are we ever going to do another Young Jean Lee or Lucas Hnath play? Probably not. Unless they are creating something in the future that I feel they couldn't make anywhere else. Artistically I feel completely in love with everything they are doing but we have to make space for artists who have yet to have those very early production experiences.

The Gate has a very similar approach – the focus is on discovering new talent rather than continuing to work with established artists. So Soho Rep and the Gate are very closely aligned in that way.

Yes, exactly. And especially when it comes to our young artists in the lab, we always try and serve as a champion and advocate for them. We almost act as agents for them in very early projects. So if something comes out of the lab that I think is amazing but is not for us, then I will try and figure out who can I get in the room that might respond. A big part of our role is trying to get artists out there.

I feel like we are in such a rich moment for playwriting currently. There's a lot of really exciting work happening and it's great to be able to share that with as many people as we can. In the UK, theatre is more accepted as a valid part of everyday life for people than it is here. So I feel a real drive to carve out space in the culture and to advocate for the vitality of theatre artists.

Do you mean that theatre is seen as having a more civic role in the UK than in the United States? After all, we have a National Theatre and the United States doesn't.

Yes. Here, theatre is something you have to really make the case for and so I feel like that's what I'm doing over and over again through the work itself and in conversation. The civic nature of theatre lies in the form itself, which is what makes it so astonishing to me. There is something about how we gather and how we experience a thing together that is transformative. Some of the shows I do are quote unquote 'political' but I'm much more interested in the form itself being a civic act than I am in content-based politics.

You're one of the few artistic directors (ADs) in New York who also regularly direct work as well – many ADs here are primarily producers or literary managers. That is very different from the UK where most ADs also direct regularly. Do you think that has an impact on how you run this building as opposed to how other organizations in New York operate?

I hear from the artists – whom we work with here – that it feels different, because they feel like they are talking to me as a peer artist. And that is definitely the dynamic I aspire to. I always make it explicit when I'm offering notes on something that they are just my opinion. I don't have any expectation that they will be implemented. In fact quite the opposite! I crave robust disagreement as that often makes the show better. I'm not interested in the 'director for hire' relationship. Though a lot of artists do end up wanting significant input and feedback, our general approach is to start from a place of transmitting autonomy to the artists and letting them tell us how we can be most helpful.

Why do you think there are fewer artistic directors in New York who actually direct as well?

Mainly because the fundraising is such a slog! The financial model in New York is completely different to the UK. I'm lucky to work with two absolutely remarkable people at the theatre: Cynthia Flowers and Meropi Peponides. Cynthia is my business partner and a phenomenal fundraiser. Meropi is an artist and a creative producer extraordinaire. Working with them has kept me sane and helped me evolve as an artist in large part because I so admire both of their work. Our board is also very pro having a working artist running the theatre, which is a rare gift. It's something that they rightly think is a big part of the DNA of the company and affects our identity and how we choose, produce and make work.

How would you define the type of community or communities that Soho Rep serves?

I used to resist this as I felt like it was hermetic, but I think I have come to accept that part of our role is to serve as a hub for people who have self-identified as theatre artists and who are trying to find their way – that up and coming generation of people who are saying: 'I think this is what I want to do with my life.' The question is, how can we serve a role in expanding the number of people who think of themselves like that? Who feels like they can self-identify as a theatre artist? It's an insane thing to do! It tends to line up with a very narrow demographic that is tightly equated with historic access to power and education.

We used to be seen as a kind of theatre speakeasy where many people never even knew we were here. But now we're more known outside just the theatre community. We've opened that up in part by developing partnerships. For example, we formed a relationship with the Borough of Manhattan Community College around five years ago. We teach classes there, we've had some of their students intern with us, and we have a programme where all of their students will come and see our work during previews. So we have forged ongoing, meaningful interactions with students who otherwise might not know what we were doing, or feel like it was for them.

Do you feel that, as an artistic director, there is a public aspect to your role?

I do, but I try and fulfil that through the work. You make the work as strongly as you can and hope that it lives in the world and seeds questions for people through the feelings they experience in the theatre. I also try to amplify the direct connection between the work and audience. That is something I've thought a lot about over the years, especially in a 'one paper town' like this where the *New York Times* is so dominant in how people understand what's being made. And, of course, I do feel like we have to make noise around the NEA[2] money getting taken away and our values being dismantled. But, generally speaking, I try and put all my energy into the work itself and have that do the speaking.

Do you think theatre has an activist role? Especially in the current context with things like Trump in the United States and Brexit in the UK?

I believe theatre has to respond to what is happening. It's a local and temporally specific medium, and it's civic in its form because it's about gathering people in a room and saying: 'Together we are all going to make this thing right now live, and you being here completes that experience.' So I feel like there's just something inherent in that form that is a kind of activism.

But do I want to commission a bunch of plays about Trump? Not interested. It's not how the theatre functions for me. I don't want to just give an audience a message and say: 'Here take this.' I want to transform how you think about yourself. What we are trying to do with the work is to destabilize people's assumptions. That's always been my interest but I feel more fired up than ever to make work that does that.

It's funny because often you will see critics in the UK say: 'The great thing about theatre is that it can respond really quickly to contemporary events.' But I just don't believe that's particularly true. It can take years to develop a really good show. By the time we have commissioned, developed, designed and produced a genuinely good show about Trump, he will probably have left office.

That's so true. The thought of creating some slapdash thing in response to Trump building a wall or whatever just doesn't interest me. We have to put our faith in pushing the ideas we're excited about and the things that make us uncomfortable. Those are going to be the things that ultimately resonate the most powerfully.

---

[2]The National Endowment for the Arts, an agency of the US Government that provides support and funding for the arts. Its entire budget was threatened by the Trump administration in 2017, though the cuts were not carried out.

Who are the artistic directors who have inspired you?

The history of the Royal Court was deeply inspiring to me when I was growing up in the UK. I ushered there and saw some plays thirty times! It was an amazing training. There's something amazing about people making a space for artists and so I always find it invigorating to learn about the history of other theatres. It's helpful sometimes to remind yourself of how unlikely it must have been for any of these things to come into existence when you're in the throes of trying to do something that often feels so impossible.

I'm really inspired by what Alec Duffy and DeeArah Wright are doing at Jack – a venue in Clinton Hill, Brooklyn. They are doing some extraordinary work with austere resources. They have made their neighbours stakeholders and co-creators in the art they do. I'm also very inspired by The Movement Theatre Company who are creating amazing work that brings together bold aesthetics and social change. I'm very excited that Maria Goyanes who used to run our Lab at Soho Rep is taking over Woolly Mammoth – which was an amazing company under Howard Shalwitz's tenure. I can't wait to see what she does!

Joe Melillo, who has run BAM[3] for a long time, is one of my mentors. What he does is a very different sort of artistic directing because it's a presenting organization. But in terms of how he thinks about relationships with artists it's actually very similar. He's been a huge force in my life. I can pick up the phone, or go and get a cup of coffee with him and talk about some impossible thing, and he always makes me feel better about it. It's so great to be able to talk to other people who have been through so much more of this crap than you have! It's a crazy job, and one of the things I'm endlessly surprised by is actually how similar the challenges are, whether it's a giant institution or a tiny theatre like ours – how do we make the work and continue to thrive and change?

---

[3]The Brooklyn Academy of Music.

2
ANDRÉ BISHOP

André Bishop was artistic director of Playwrights Horizons in New York City throughout the 1980s. Situated on 42nd Street, Playwrights Horizons is one of the leading producers of new American plays in the United States. He became artistic director of Lincoln Center Theater (LCT) in New York in 1992. LCT is home to the Vivian Beaumont Theater, a large-scale Broadway house, and the Mitzi E. Newhouse Theater, a smaller-scale studio.

How did you come to be artistic director first of Playwrights Horizons and then of Lincoln Center Theater?

I have absolutely no idea how I ended up in this job or in my job at Playwrights Horizons. I never set out to be an artistic director or a producer or anything like that, though I've always lived a life where the only thing I'm really interested in is the theatre. I was lucky enough to grow up in New York City and lucky enough to be taken to the theatre at a very young age. There's this book called *Act One* by Moss Hart; it's the greatest book ever written about how a young man gets into theatre. One of the opening sentences says: 'The theatre is the first refuge of the unhappy child.' And I was certainly that. So all I ever wanted to do, based, I suppose, on my inner feelings about the world when I was young, was be in the theatre.

I started out thinking I wanted to be an actor, when I was at school. I suppose that's what everyone thinks they will do in the beginning. When I got out of college I moved back to New York and I did lots of odd jobs in those first few years. I taught French, I worked at a publishing house, I worked for a record company – a lot of different things. But I wasn't very happy. So I went and studied acting privately with two different men:

Fred Kareman and Wynn Handman who were both disciples of Sanford Meisner who's one of the founders of The Neighborhood Playhouse.

Wynn Handman ran a theatre called The American Place Theater, which has been closed for many years now. But in its day, it was an experimental place that introduced writers from other mediums into the theatre. So a lot of poets and novelists wrote plays there. He was a great teacher, and he often worked on new texts with his students, which was quite unusual. He really knew how to analyse a scene and break it down from an actor's point of view.

Anyway, I started acting and I got some jobs, but I was still not happy. It wasn't that I was a bad actor. I think I was actually quite good, but I had no confidence. I loved being on stage, but everything before that filled me with terror. I was quite happy in the shadows and very happy in the spotlight, but getting from one to the other was virtually crippling to me.

Then, in the early 1970s, I met this guy, Bob Moss, who had just founded Playwrights Horizons. Broadway was no longer that hospitable to new American writing or to young writers. So all these non-profit, institutional theatres had started up here – of which Playwrights was one. And I said to him: 'I don't know what I want to do'. He said: 'Just come here and do whatever you want.' So I went there and I answered the phone, cleaned the bathrooms and made myself generally useful. There was a staff of three of us at that point and we had just moved into this seedy old burlesque house on West 42nd Street. At the time this was a block filled with failed or failing porn palaces and there was still some prostitution going on in the street. But the rent was cheap and we renovated it cheaply, and we just started putting on plays. The mission in those days was to fan every flame – so we did around fifteen small productions of new plays a year, with new directors and new designers. And even though the area between 9th and 10th Avenues was very dangerous, audiences came. We charged no admission but we held out a bag for contributions at the end of every show. No one got paid in those days.

And there was this huge pile of unopened manila envelopes because people had been mailing in plays. And Bob had been so busy starting this other theatre in Queens that no one had read them. So I went to him and said: 'We're called Playwrights Horizons, but we're not reading anything. We've got stacks of unopened manuscripts. Could I read some of them and write you reports?' And he said yes, so I started doing just that and became one of the first literary managers in this country. I started meeting a younger generation of writers and putting on readings and so on. At the same time, I was still acting but I reached one of those moments in life where you have make a decision. I'd been cast in a tour of Alan Bennett's play *Habeas Corpus*. It was the kind of role that I always played: a sensitive, neurotic young person. It was a fairly long commitment – around half a year. But I thought: 'I've made myself almost indispensable to this new theatre. If I leave, that could all go away, I might not be able to come back.' So I turned the part down and decided I would stop acting, and I never thought about it again.

So I started being full-time at Playwrights Horizons and eventually became the artistic director. I'm leaving out endless amounts of stuff, but essentially I was the right person at the right time in the right place. This wasn't because I'm so great but because my evolution as a theatre person was parallel to the evolution of Playwrights Horizons as a theatre, which was parallel to the growth of the non-profit theatre movement. That could never happen today because everything has gotten much more sophisticated. When we were at Playwrights we were learning on our feet. We had no management in the beginning. We didn't have press agents or any of that stuff. We, and a few others, had set out clearly to be an alternative to the commercial theatre. In fact, in the first charter of Playwrights Horizons, I remember it saying that we were devoted to the support, development and production of new American playwrights as an alternative to the commercial theatre.

When I became head of Playwrights Horizons, things had been very up and down. We'd done a lot of plays and were about ten years into its evolution. I'd been there for six or seven years, and we were in terrible financial shape. The theatre that Bob Moss had created in Queens, which was a large subscription house that did old plays and was supposed to financially support the work of the new plays in Manhattan, was collapsing. There was a big gas shortage at the time and many of the subscribers could no longer drive to the theatre because gas was rationed. Bob and I took a walk and he said: 'Look, I'm too tired. I don't want to do this anymore. We can either shake hands and say, "It's been great, we helped a lot of people, we were a useful theatre but now we'll close." Or you can take over and do whatever you want with it.'

So I thought about it for really a very short amount of time and decided that I would give it a go. Again, it was a fluke – my whole career has been a kind of fluke. I decided to narrow down the scope and focus of the theatre. We did fewer plays, we did them better and we then had four enormously successful shows in a row. We did a musical called *March of the Falsettos*; then we did a play by Chris Durang called *Sister Mary Ignatius Explains It All for You*; then there was hugely successful play by A. R. Gurney called *The Dining Room*; and then we did a play by Wendy Wasserstein called *Isn't It Romantic*. We also got a press agent, so people started writing about us. And we developed a more committed and more generous board and we took off. We grew and grew and grew, and it became what it is today: a leading off-Broadway theatre devoted to new writing.

And so then you came to Lincoln Center Theater?
Yes. That was the early 1990s. The history of this theatre, up until my predecessors Gregory Mosher and Bernard Gersten took over, had basically been one of unmitigated disaster. There had been many administrations and none of them had really been able to make sense of it. There were massive in-fighting between Lincoln Center Inc and this theatre, an inability to come to terms with the Beaumont stage and to deal with the architecture of a thrust theatre, and massive financial challenges.Though I must say that while the other demons have long gone away, the financial challenges have not. Anyway, after four and a half years Gregory decided to leave and they needed someone quickly, and I guess I was the kind of golden boy of the New York theatre.

Because Playwrights was doing so well?
Yes, and they didn't want to spend a lot of time looking. I never thought I would ever leave Playwrights Horizons, which had grown so beautifully and which I loved with all my heart and soul. It never occurred to me to leave, and certainly not for Lincoln Center, which I had misgivings about. I wasn't sure about the thrust stage and the uptown vibe – with all the marble! But I didn't interview; I just got offered the job. I thought: 'I'm not really ready to leave this theatre that I love so much. But these opportunities don't happen often. If I decide not to take this job, I may never get another job.' I mean, I would have loved to run The Public Theater, but I never would have gotten that job because even at

Playwrights Horizons I would have been considered much too uptown and too establishment.

So I left Playwrights, which was very difficult, emotionally, for them and for me, and came here. I came because I wanted to do the classics. My experience was in working with new writers, and, of course, we do huge amounts of new work here, but I wanted to do more than that. I'm drawn to plays with very idiosyncratic language and with enormously meaty wonderful roles. I love bravura acting and I love bravura writing.

You need those bravura roles to fill a space like the Beaumont presumably?

Yes. The Beaumont is one of the greatest theatre spaces in the world if it is used well. The problem with it is you can't do everything in it. It doesn't work particularly well for naturalistic family dramas. And it doesn't work particularly well for farce because you need people to all be looking in the same direction. But it works wonderfully well for presentational plays, for plays of great language like Shakespeare, or for monologists like Spalding Gray. And it works extremely well for serious, large musicals because it is the third largest stage space in New York after the Met Opera and Radio City. And what it has is the ability to have both epic scale and intimacy because the last row isn't very far from the stage.

So how do you go about programming the Beaumont?

We're very lucky here because we don't have subscribers. We just have members who pay a small fee and get first dibs on the best seats. And that means we don't have to promise to produce a specific number of plays a year. And because they don't pay in advance, if they're not interested in seeing whatever play or musical we're doing, they don't have to buy a ticket. So there are times when we do, maybe, seven or eight plays in a year. And there are years when we might only do four plays. So for a theatre this big, we are remarkably mobile and adaptable.

What was interesting to me when I came here is that there was nothing particularly corporate about Lincoln Center Theater. We had no publicly stated lofty ideals. Part of the problem with the old regimes is that they had made these insane pronouncements that this was going to be the United States' national theatre and so on. But when Bernie and

Gregory came here, they had their motto: 'good plays, popular prices'. That was it. They made no lofty pronouncements or promises beyond that. And I was very happy about that.

The result is that I never plan seasons. We had one year where the only things we did were musicals. And if we have a show that is successful like *South Pacific* or *War Horse*, then we keep it running. But those shows are not picked for that reason. People told me I was insane to do *South Pacific*. Those shows have saved us, financially, but I never think about that stuff. I never had to at Playwrights Horizons, and I've never done so here.

I've been lucky enough to kind of do what I want with the writers whom I want. I've never thought: 'Will the audience like it?' I've only thought: 'Will I like it?' And sometimes things work out wonderfully, and sometimes they disappoint. But this theatre is quite loose and we have a lot of projects that have just started out of the blue.

Tell me about your audience here. Is it true to say that they are predominantly wealthy, white and older?

I think that the idea about Lincoln Center Theater being this bastion of privilege and elitism is very much receding. And it's receding because for the most part it isn't true. It may be true that the Metropolitan Opera audience is wealthy, white and older. But while our audience here is predominantly white and older, they're certainly not wealthy. They're Upper West Side liberals basically. Our tickets are really still quite cheap, and we have a huge under-thirty-five programme. We have 38,000 members who can get good seats to any play for $30.

And what are your thoughts on diversifying the theatre more generally?

Diversifying the work is easier than diversifying the audience, though one will inevitably and eventually lead to the other. There's no question in my mind that we have hugely diversified our work in the past four or five years. Not just in terms of ethnic considerations but also in terms of gender. We've won awards three years in a row for the gender parity we have achieved. We have many women writing plays, and many women directing them and directing plays by men. This year, for instance, we're doing three plays in the Mitzi. One was written by a man and directed by a man, and the other two were written and directed by women. But

I'm not someone who is comfortable discussing this stuff. I believe in just doing it rather than endlessly talking about it.

I also think that the diversification of our staff is an absolute necessity, but it's going to take a while. There are very few African American designers in the American theatre, for example, and without wanting to sound condescending, something has to be done about that. But I think theatres across the country are changing very rapidly in this area, and changing for the good.

Artistic directors often have quite an important role to play in terms of public advocacy either for the building they run or for the industry as a whole. Do you see yourself as having a public role in terms of the wider conversation?
I don't think I am a public figure. I think it's very different in London, where the person who runs the National is certainly a public figure, and actually many artistic directors there are. Though I guess that might be the case for some people here, I'm sure Oskar Eustis at The Public considers himself to be a spokesperson and civic and social leader. And in many ways he is; that's his personality. He's a very political animal and has a very deep and profound activist social conscience – he's thoroughly admirable in that way. I don't have that kind of confidence, to be honest, though I have confidence in what I do in my world, and I speak about that all the time. I love the theatre and everything about it; it has been my entire life.

So I suppose I am an advocate for this theatre, and God knows, I'm an advocate for the non-profit theatre, which I believe in totally as a movement and as the chief cultural force in this country. I do get asked from time to time to give my opinion on the theatre to a newspaper. I'm proud of what all the theatres in this country do. We are in a golden age of the American theatre and of the new American play. We just don't know it because most of us are so neurotic that we can't see straight. We think: 'Oh my God, this is wrong and that is wrong.' But despite the lack of subsidy from the government, this country is just blooming with theatre and much of it very good.

How do you think the theatre will or should respond to Trump?
I think it's too early to tell. People ask me: 'Well, what are "your" writers going to do? What are they writing about? Are they writing about

Trump?' And I always say: 'I hope they're not writing about Trump yet.' I mean at this point it's only been two-and-a-half months of horror. And in New York, you're only preaching to the converted anyway if you do a play about some evil man with dyed hair, who calls women horrible names. *Saturday Night Live* does that.

But what I do think with all my being is that in bad times the theatre becomes more important than ever. That is what I hear from audiences. They either want to go out and get away from their woes and worries, or they want to see a play that somehow has meaning in the larger context. So I think audiences need the theatre more than ever because of what's going on in this country.

It will be interesting to see, in the coming years, what all of this does in terms of playwriting. I mean, this isn't the Weimar Republic; we're not at a point where it's like the Soviet Union and all satirical things must be hidden and made as metaphor. We can still write whatever we want to. But I do think people want to come together to see something provoking or just comforting more than I can remember in a long time. I've also noticed the degree of attention that the audience pays to a play and the degree of enthusiasm with which they greet it is far greater than it used to be.

Finally, who are the artistic directors, past or present, whom you admire?

Well, I admired a man named Ellis Rabb who ran the APA Repertory Company. That was the Association of Producing Artists. They started in Michigan and then they came to New York where they merged with the Phoenix Theatre. They were a true rep company. Ellis was an actor and a director and he was a real man of the theatre. I only knew him towards the end of his life, but I admired what he did. I also admired Eva Le Gallienne, who was a great actress, who founded the Civic Repertory Theatre in New York City.

I admire all those founders of the non-profit movement. Joe Papp terrified me – he could be very brusque and scary – but I admired his social conscience, his energy, his civic mindedness and his liberal viewpoints. And, of course, there was Zelda Fichandler who started the Arena Stage in Washington DC, Gordon Davidson at Center Theatre Group in Los Angeles and Ellen Stewart with her wacky way of just taking all these talented people in at La MaMa here in New York. And nowadays, of course, I admire Oskar Eustis and Jim Nicola. And in England I know Richard Eyre quite well and I admired him a lot and, of course, I admire Nick Hytner.

There's not a single person I can think of whom I don't admire. What they do and the way they do it may not be the way I would do it, but who cares? I think I admire anyone who has a vision and can carry it out and inspire others to do the same. I'm less concerned about the specifics of that vision. Whenever I speak to young directors, I always say the same thing: 'You have to stick to your principles, and you must stick with your aesthetic, but all I ask is that you be open to the principles and the aesthetics and the feelings and the beliefs of others. There is not one way of making theatre. There's your way, and you can do it your way, but you have to be open to others.' It's a profession that requires generosity. You can only excel at it if you work very hard, and think very carefully, and are, yourself, very generous.

3
OSKAR EUSTIS

Oskar Eustis was artistic director of the Eureka Theater in San Francisco and then from 1994 to 2005 of Trinity Repertory Company in Rhode Island. He has been artistic director of The Public Theater in New York since 2005. The Public houses five performance spaces ranging from 99 to 299 seats. It also produces Shakespeare in the Park every summer at the open-air Delacorte Theater in Central Park.

Tell me about your journey to becoming artistic director of The Public.

I come from a politically radical family. My parents were communists, which is very rare over here. My first march on Washington was when I was ten years old in 1969 – against the Vietnam War. In the early 1970s, the mix of political and cultural radicalism was extremely anarchistic and crazy. It was a period in our country where being politically left and culturally progressive were all part of this stew of culture and politics and sex and drugs, and the counter-cultural lifestyle.

On the wave of that, when I was sixteen in 1975, I came to New York – having graduated from high school early. I came here as a leftie hippie who was completely enamoured of the avant-garde: Grotowski, The Living Theatre, The Performance Group and Mabou Mines. I actually lived at the Performing Garage down on Wooster Street. And I walked into The Public for the first time as a Mabou Mines groupie because they were in residence here. So The Public imprinted on me, at a very early age, the ideal of what a theatre should be.

Also, around that time I'd had my last ever audition as an actor for Joe Papp, which went terribly! I literally walked out of the room and said I'd never audition again, and I became a director. So I founded a company called the Red Wing Theater Company, which made completely obscure, avant-garde, experimental work. It had some modest success in this country. My co-artistic director was a Swiss gentleman Stefan Muller, who became my best friend. And then lo and behold, we were hired by the Schauspielhaus Zürich to found an experimental second stage for them, called Das Labor – the Laboratory, which still exists today.

But finally, I had this huge crisis of conscience. Two things did it. Patti Smith released her album *Easter* and in it she has a song called 'Babelogue' in which she sings: 'In heart, in heart, in heart I am a Muslim. In heart, in heart, I am an American artist, and I have no guilt.' I heard this and I just started weeping but I didn't know why. Then I read an article in *Yale Theater Magazine* from Joan Holden, who was the chief writer for the San Francisco Mime Troupe, and the first sentence was: 'We are a theatre that does not hold its audience in contempt.' I stayed up all night after reading that. I realized that everything I was doing in Switzerland was basically trying to intimidate the audience into thinking I was smarter than they were. While that was giving my ego gratification, it meant I didn't have anything to say to them that mattered. I realized that the entire enterprise had become completely corrupt. It wasn't anybody else's fault – just mine. I was doing it for all the wrong reasons.

The separation between my politics and my art had become unbearable. I wasn't speaking to the audience whom I should be speaking to. I wasn't talking about the subjects that I should be talking about. It had become completely rarefied. I also read an essay by Roland Barthes from the 1950s, called 'Who's Theatre? Who's Avant-Garde?' It's a beautiful essay that, basically, makes the case that the avant-garde, far from being counter-cultural, is actually a necessary prop for bourgeois culture. At the time, that was a radical idea for me. Nowadays it seems obvious, but back then it was really a stunning idea. So the ideological underpinnings of my life fell apart at the age of twenty or twenty-one.

I returned to New York and was completely lost. It was 1980 and the city didn't look like it had looked when I'd last lived there. So I tumbled into San Francisco. Raymond Chandler said that they tipped the country on end and everyone with a screw loose fell into California. My company, Red Wing, had done a residency there in 1978 at a little theatre called the Eureka and the town had very generously embraced us. So I went back there. There was nobody there that I'd known from before, but I walked in and said: 'I think I should work here.' I'd saved enough from Switzerland so that I could afford to work there for about two years, without making any money. By the time the two years was up, I had a salary and I was the resident director and dramaturge and then later I became artistic director. That ten years I spent at the Eureka was really when I grew up. It moulded me, and I moulded it. The first play that I commissioned and dramaturged there was Emily Mann's *Execution of Justice* which was a big success and was also a huge turning point for me. Then, of course, while I was still at the Eureka, I commissioned Mr Kushner to write *Angels in America*.

And that did okay!

Yes! What it meant was that by 1989, I was thirty-one and I was kind of a grown-up. My dad had just died, I'd broken up with my girlfriend and the Eureka was starting to fall apart. My partner there, Tony Taccone who had run the theatre with me for the last decade, had moved on and was the associate artistic director at Berkeley Rep, where he's still working. *Angels* was coming along beautifully, but it became apparent to me that the Eureka didn't have enough money or resources to produce it. And in the mid of this kind of crisis of confidence, Gordon Davidson, who was the artistic director of the Mark Taper Forum in LA, offered me a job as associate artistic director. I was completely flummoxed because I had never thought of myself as having a career in that way – I was just doing work. I had been this passionate avant-gardist who turned into a member of the Eureka Theater Collective. Yet suddenly, for the first time, I had to think of myself as a completely free agent, who could be hired by somebody else. I had a really hard time deciding what to do about it, until my friend, Burke Walker, who at that time ran the Empty Space in Seattle, said to me: 'Ask yourself where you can be of the most use.' It was a brilliant question for me because it allowed me to think about my career without being a careerist. For a commie kid, that was really necessary. And it became clear to me that I should take *Angels* to the Taper because we could finish it there. That was where I could be of use. The reason all of this mattered is because it was part of the gradual change from my primary identity being as a director, to my primary identity being as a dramaturge and then as an artistic director or producer.

If my life had worked out exactly the way I wanted it to, I would have been Peter Brook. I would have been the most revered director of my lifetime. But what became clear to me is that the place where my talents were most of use was as a dramaturge and as an artistic director. I was most brought to life by the possibility of supporting, encouraging, nurturing, challenging and making real other artist's visions – that was my calling.

So how did you arrive at The Public?
I spent five years at the Taper – it was the only time I really worked for somebody else. I learned an enormous amount there, both from Gordon directly and from just operating within a large, regional theatre. I was then headhunted to go run Trinity Rep in Providence, Rhode Island. So at the age of thirty-five I took that job, and that turned out to be exactly the right thing for me. I spent an incredibly happy decade there. And then the Taper artistic director job opened up because Gordon was retiring. They headhunted me and I went into that process and came very close to taking it. But then I had this realization. I thought: 'You know what? The main reason I'm taking this job is that if The Public Theater opened up right now, I don't think I would be the top candidate. But if I ran the Taper successfully for a few years, then I would be the top candidate.' And I thought: 'What a lousy reason to take a job just because it's going to position you for the job you really want.' So I didn't take it. And to my great surprise, about eighteen months later, George Wolfe announced he was stepping down from The Public. This is the only job that I've ever actively sought and I had to go after it tooth and nail because I was right – I was not on the top list of candidates! So I set out to demonstrate to them that I understood what this theatre stood for. I know its history like the back of my hand. I was forty-four so for thirty years it had been my most beloved theatre. I had just absorbed its history through my pores. Joe Papp was a member of the Communist Party. So that idea of a socially radical artistic director who, like me, never went to college and was sort of an auto-didact, coming in and running this place, was fundamentally comfortable for the board and they hired me. And it's been hard, but I've not regretted for a moment.

And how much do you think this building has shaped you, and how much do you think you've been able to shape it?
This is the only theatre that I could imagine running in which I found no need to change one iota of its mission. I was shaped by its mission as

a young man and so there's no air between what this theatre stands for and what I stand for. It has a radically democratic mission resting on the idea that culture belongs to everybody, and that everybody has a story to tell and should be able to tell it. That means that access is key. Not just access for audience, although that's hugely important, but also access for artists, access for communities without a voice to tell their own story.

I don't feel like I've changed the place. Rather, what I've done is figure out how to execute its mission in the most artistically vibrant and exciting way I can. I've reached back in to the theatre's history in order to find a way of looking forward. One image that I've used sometimes is that I'm Brigham Young, not Joseph Smith. I'm not the charismatic founder of the Church of Latter Day Saints. I'm the guy who, once the founder has gone, tries to build it into a structure that will last forever. The Public has had three geniuses before me as artistic directors: Joe Papp, JoAnne Akalaitis and George Wolfe. I don't think I'm a genius, but I do think I'm a builder, the first professional artistic director The Public has ever had. None of the others had ever been an artistic director before. So I think I've been able to build up the systems. We are literally four times as large as we were when I got here eleven years ago. We had a $12 million budget and now we're at $48 million. That's not because of my vision changing the mission. That's my ability to execute the mission that Joe already laid down, in a successful way.

You've talked about access but a ticket for a show here can cost up to $120, and obviously that's quite a barrier. How do you find the balance between making the money at the box office that you need to survive and still keeping the work as accessible as possible for communities that can't afford those prices?

The primary way is that we do a number of programmes that are free. Free Shakespeare in the park is the flagship of that. We give away 100,000 tickets every year for nothing. We also have the mobile unit which tours around all the boroughs. We go to prisons, we go to halfway houses, we go right to the places where people don't have access to culture and that's completely free. The first preview of every show done here in the main building is free. There are lotteries where there are $10 tickets for every show we do.

But none of that is adequate. I will not be happy until all of our shows downtown are free, the way the Delacorte is. And we've actually got plans to move towards that. It's not an insurmountable barrier and I think that will be a game changer. The idea behind it is exactly the same as the idea behind free public lending libraries – the theatre belongs to everybody: it's your birthright. This building started as the New York public library in the 1940s. It was a fairly radical idea that anybody should be able to go in and walk out with a book that they get to read for free. But, at a cultural level, we decided that was important for the democratization of literature. We can make that same decision for the theatre. If we're able to pull that off, what a shot it would be across the bow of the whole market economy. That would be a huge game changer. I'm relatively confident we'll be able to do that before I die.

And how would that work with a major commercial musical like *Hamilton*, which started its life here?
Well, there we fly right into the belly of the beast. *Hamilton* is this thing where the most democratic and inclusive of shows has become the most exotic commodity that you can imagine. Figuring out how to navigate that is complicated. The basic thing we're doing, of course, is redistributing the wealth. Everything The Public gets from *Hamilton* goes into subsidizing work that is accessible. I'm very proud of the high school programme in which we provide tickets to students for $10, which we are now replicating in Chicago and San Francisco. But the thing that I'm advocating for, and I still have to completely convince my partners, is I want to release the rights to perform it to high schools. My thought is that for the next twenty years, the only way you can see *Hamilton* is to see one of our productions, or to see your local high school doing it. And I just think that would change the fucking world. Imagine what it would do to urban high schools – how it would help the history teachers, the drama teachers. By doing this we would be saying to young performers across the country: 'The theatre is the hippest place to be.' That's what's going to really change who writes for the theatre and who participates in the theatre. Right now it's not the hippest thing to do when you're a teenager.

In relation to that, The Public Works Program is the one thing that I would say indisputably I've added to the armament here. It's our large-scale, public participatory pageant that we do every Labor Day. We partner with community organizations in each of the five boroughs and work with them year round – doing classes, giving them free tickets, etc. Then, once a year, we audition all those participants for a huge pageant on the stage of the Delacorte as part of Shakespeare in the Park. It's a musicalized version of Shakespeare, written by some of our best musical theatre artists. We have five equity actors, the best New York has, and 240 community members. The shows have been incandescently brilliant. Not just good for the people doing them, but for the audience. They are my favourite performance events of the year.

That barrier of professional and non-professional sets up a binary: 'I'm an artist, you're a consumer of art.' I want to break that down. The thesis of Public Works is that it's not a binary; it's not that you either are or aren't an artist. Everybody is an artist. Some people have gotten to spend more of their lives doing it, and have trained more, and are more skilled at it, and some people have gotten to spend less of their lives doing it, but it's a gradation. It's not absolute. The revolutionary impact that has had is huge. It's now being imitated across the country – in Dallas, Seattle and so on. We're trying to create a national movement that says that the distinction between professional and non-professional is not the fortress on which we should make our stand. We should actually let a thousand flowers bloom. As we would have said in my youth!

Well, that's definitely a way to persuade Trump to fund it!
Yes, by quoting Mao! You know, I'm the only artistic director with a hand-carved statue of Lenin in his office. Other people have Tony awards on their shelf. Nobody else has a hand-carved statue of Lenin!

In terms of programming the theatre, how do you go about choosing artist and projects?
Except for rapid response projects, which sometimes we can do like lightning, developing a project can take anywhere from two to six years before we put it on. So I programme my season based on what projects are ready. But in terms of how we decide what to develop, well, you work with artists who you really believe in, who are dealing with subject matter or content that you think is important. Because we are the Public, it means that in general we work on public plays. An example I use is Shakespeare. There's no such thing as a private relationship in

Shakespeare. If two people fall in love, their parents are immediately involved. Their society is immediately involved. Their prince is involved. Which is actually like real life. It's just that somehow in our storytelling culture we've decided to pretend that we have private lives that aren't connected to those things. So we do Shakespeare and we do new plays that are inspired by that same kind of thinking: that our private lives are actually enmeshed with our public lives.

Also, we are constantly trying to push the boundaries of who gets to tell their story. That means diversity is not something we 'apply' to the season; it is at the core of what we have to do. So *of course* we have different ethnicities telling their story; *of course* we worry about gender balance all of the time. And now because the issue is really coming to a head, we're trying to grapple directly with transgender issues. I think we were the first theatre in the country to make gender-neutral bathrooms. But you also have to deal with that in the content of what's on stage. The question 'who tells their story?' is key. You've got to give people the right to not only tell their story but for their story to be seen as central to the American story. One of the things that's so special about The Public, something I have loved about it since my teenage years, is that it's a big tent. We do Shakespeare, we do new plays, we do new musicals, we do cabaret, we do experimental work, we do Public Works. By doing them all together, we're saying: 'Listen. All of this work is part of the American theatre community. I'm not interested in siloing it or segregating it.' And that is the same as what the United States is supposed to say – the promise of the United States is we're all part of it.

Who are the artistic directors who have inspired you in the past or whom you look to now?

Peter Stein at the Schaubühne was my hero when I was young. I thought what he was doing there in the 1970s and 1980s was one of the great theatrical experiments of our time. Ariane Mnouchkine at Théâtre Du Soleil in Paris is inspiring – though we have completely different theatre systems so I can't really imitate her. Martha Lavey, who for many years was artistic director at Steppenwolf, was somebody I admired enormously and I also love Anna Shapiro who has replaced her. What Bob Falls did in Chicago in terms of how he organized his artistic staff was very inspiring to me. Tyrone Guthrie was a huge influence on me. I grew up in Minneapolis, and watching what he did at that theatre as well as what one of his successors, Garland Wright, did was incredibly inspiring. Nowadays, I'm a big friend and fan of Rufus Norris at the National and of David Lan – he did wonderful work at the Young Vic. With Rufus I think he is still searching for his complete legitimation, but that comes. That's the thing – you get the job and then you earn the job and that usually takes about three years. It was about three years into my time here before people really said: 'Yes, he's the artistic director of the Public.' And Rufus is still in that process, but I think he is genuinely a great guy. Daldry was also incredibly exciting at the Royal Court back in the old days – I've always loved the Court but that was a particularly fecund period.

4
PAIGE EVANS

Paige Evans was artistic director of LCT3 at the Lincoln Center from 2008 to 2016. LCT3 is dedicated to new writers, new directors and new designers. She was appointed as artistic director of Signature Theatre in 2016. Signature has three performance spaces in its home on West 42nd Street and is dedicated to being an artistic home for playwrights.

Could you tell me about your journey to becoming artistic director at Signature Theatre?

I grew up in New York City and my parents were theatregoers. They took me to a ton of theatres growing up, and that's how I got to love it. Like many people who work on the producing side of things in theatre, I started as an actor and acted all the way through high school. In college, I studied playwriting.

After that, I moved to Italy for a few years and taught at an international high school and was the arts editor of a newspaper and then backpacked around Southeast Asia for a year. But eventually I decided that I wanted to go into theatre, as it was a passion for me throughout my life.

I met with Lynne Meadow at Manhattan Theatre Club (when it was a much smaller organization), whom I knew through a mutual friend. She had me read some plays and then she created a job for me as artistic assistant. It became clear to me that the literary department was where my interests and skills really lay, so I worked my way up through that department for about six years.

Then I did a fellowship in Cuba for two years. It was a self-designed travel, study and writing fellowship with the Institute of Current World Affairs. Every year they pay for two young Americans to go anywhere in the world and study anything they want. I was one of the rare applicants who were interested in the arts. So I went to Cuba and studied the performing arts: music, theatre and dance; and I met with a lot of artists and interviewed them and wrote about them each month. It was fascinating. Then Lynne brought me back to Manhattan Theatre Club as associate artistic director.

I then became the first artistic director of LCT3 at Lincoln Center Theater. The thing that has run through all of these jobs, for me, is new writing and working with playwrights. At LCT3, my job was to find writers who were new to Lincoln Center Theater. Our tagline was: 'New artists, new audiences'. The mission was to bring new artists to Lincoln Center Theater, give them full productions at LCT3 and then hopefully have them work on the larger stages there over time. It worked well. There were a lot of directors, designers and stage managers who made the leap, as well as some writers. For instance, we transferred Amy Herzog's *4,000 Miles* from LCT3 to the Mitzi E. Newhouse Theatre.

The other half of the mission was to bring in new audiences to Lincoln Center Theater, through LCT3, and then hopefully have them see shows on the other stages too. That was a challenge. I had to try to find artists who I thought could work at Lincoln Center Theater but who also might bring in younger, more ethnically, socio-economically and generationally diverse audiences.

Presumably the lower ticket prices at LCT3 helped with that too?

Yes, they were $25 for my first seven years, and then we made it $30 in my last year there. And we just did the same thing here at Signature. The tickets were $25 for a long time and then we just raised them to $30.

So how did you end up here at Signature?

Jim Houghton[1] sent an email to people within the theatre community letting everyone know that he was stepping down because of his illness and that a great job was opening up. And it was something that interested me. I loved my job at LCT3, and so to leave it, I had to feel like I was taking a great next step to a theatre that would be a good fit

[1]James Houghton was the founding artistic director of Signature Theatre Company. He died in 2016.

for me and I for it. Signature, because it's so oriented around the writer, felt right, and, of course, the ticket prices were similar to what we had at LCT3.

While it's still early days for me here, I want to stay true to the core mission, which is special and which attracted me to come here. And that is the commitment to the playwright over a series of plays, not just one play. For instance, with Suzan-Lori Parks, we're producing four of her plays over one year. Suzan-Lori is a *Residency One* playwright, and RES1 is something that Signature has been doing for twenty-five years.

And those can be extant plays; they don't have to be new presumably?

Exactly. But when Signature moved to this new building, they had many more spaces and expanded the mission to add *Residency Five* – which is more oriented towards new work. That involves a commitment on our part to producing three premieres over five years, though five years is a somewhat ambitious goal. The only person who's done it is Will Eno, who just finished his third piece here. It can take more than five years to deliver three plays. We have two offices that are for our resident playwrights. Some, like Branden Jacobs-Jenkins, really use them and some don't, but the point is for them to feel that this is their artistic home.

We just announced the first four writers of my tenure. The first RES1 is Stephen Adly Guirgis. We're starting next season with his play *Jesus Hopped the 'A' Train* and then will produce *Our Lady of 121st Street* in the spring and a new play the following season. Lynn Nottage is going to be the RES1 playwright the following season. We'll produce two existing plays of Lynn's next season and then a new play by Lynn the following fall. And then the first of the two RES5 playwrights that I'm bringing to Signature is Dominique Morisseau.

She's great! We did the world premiere of her play *Sunset Baby* at the Gate.

I loved *Sunset Baby*. We're going to start with the New York premiere of her play *Paradise Blue* – which is set in 1940s Detroit. Dave Malloy is the other RES5 writer I am bringing in. He will be our first composer-in-residence, and his shows will be the first musicals at Signature.

That's interesting – working with a composer kind of expands the idea of what counts as a writer, doesn't it? Why shouldn't a writer of music be considered in the same way as a writer of words?

Exactly. Dave writes the book, music and lyrics for his musicals, so there is a strong and unified authentic voice. These are all writers with whom I've collaborated with in one way or another at the other theatres where I've worked, so I have a working relationship with them already. I'm very excited about continuing to work with them. I loved my job at LCT3, but because of the mission there, I was only able to work with a writer once or maybe twice. Here at Signature, we work with writers over a series of productions, which I love.

And writers are excited about coming here. They are drawn both to the idea of having an artistic home where there's a commitment to their body of work, and they are attracted to our audience. Dominique has said that Signature's Ticket Initiative, where all tickets are $30, means a lot to her – it means that friends of hers and younger people can come and see her plays without having to spend a huge amount of money.

And what is the third residency?

That is the Legacy Residency that involves bringing writers back after they've finished a RES1 or RES5. For example, Signature produced Arthur Miller's *Incident at Vichy* last year. And next year, if all goes according to plan, we will do a play by Edward Albee. Every once in a while, we will bring back either a RES1 or a RES5 writer, who has finished their residency. For instance, after Athol Fugard finished his RES1, Jim brought him back twice in a row. And that is a nice thing to be able to add to the mix.

We've touched on the cheap ticket prices at Signature Theatre already. And it feels to me that that is one of the most significant aspects of Jim Houghton's legacy here – because ticket prices in New York are usually astronomically high – much higher even than in London. So how different does that make the audience feel here? What impact has that had on the energy of the building?

It's definitely different compared to the other two institutional theatres where I've worked: MTC and the Lincoln Center Theater. They both have fairly typical institutional theatre-going audiences which are older, white, fairly well-to-do people. And we certainly have those kinds of avid theatre goers here as well. But based on our current season at least, we have a much more diverse audience, socio-economically, generationally and racially.

The Signature Ticket Initiative makes a huge difference. So many people have said to me that it really allows them to see high-quality theatre for an affordable price. But it is a funding challenge. We have to get it underwritten. Our biggest funder is Pershing Square, which our building's named after, and they've committed, through to 2031, to underwrite half of what it costs us to have the ticket subsidy. So we have to raise the other half.

And, of course, the architecture of this building is really important. When Jim showed me round a few years ago, he made the point that it had been designed to be democratic – so actors and audiences come in through the same doors and share the same space. And it's one of the very few theatres in New York that have public spaces open during the day where you can just sit and work. You can't do that in a lot of theatres here.

Yes, it's very community-oriented. That was a big part of Jim's thinking and planning, and it helps make this an exciting place to be.

Do you think that atmosphere impacts upon how the writers approach their work or how the directors and the artists making work here approach what they do?

A number of artists who have been here this season have said to me that the sense of community feels very real. A lot of people in the theatre community come during the day and have meetings, get work done or use the Wi-Fi. There is a feeling to this place that's very open and accessible. People can come in and they don't have to buy something at the cafe if they don't want to; they can just sit at one of the tables.

Another thing that Jim planned is that all of the curtains happen at the same time. So the audience are all in the lobby at the same time before the shows and oftentimes afterwards. And that is exciting. There are not many places in New York where you feel there are all these different people coming to see different things and mixing together. It feels very dynamic, and I love that.

What draws you to a particular writer?

It's been different at each of the places that I've worked because of the different nature of each organization's mission. But I think taste is extremely individual. I guess I'm looking for things that feel fresh or exciting to me, and I try to programme an eclectic range of work. I hope to produce work where the audience might go out afterwards and talk about it. That was one of the things to me that was really exciting about Ayad Akhtar's *Disgraced*. People wanted to talk about the play after seeing it.

How much of a role does the press play in your sense of what you do? Do you think about how they might respond to the things you programme?

You never know how they will react, so I try to not think about that. With new work particularly, there's almost always a spectrum of opinions. Sometimes it's all negative or all positive but most of the time it's a pretty broad range of individual responses. So I try not to second-guess it. But it does have an impact. The *New York Times* will have an impact on whether a play gets regional productions. Thankfully though, reviews no longer have as much of an influence on single ticket buyers, especially younger people. Social media and word-of-mouth play a much stronger role, especially with $30 tickets.

How big is your subscriber audience?

About 6,000. We try to keep it to less than 50 per cent of our ticket buyers for a regular run. They're very important, but we want to make sure single ticket buyers are also able to get the $30 tickets. I'd say we are less vulnerable to reviews here because of the $30 tickets and the fact that we have smaller houses. But reviews still do have an impact – more so on the writers than on anything else.

Reviews can make artists feel very vulnerable. At the Gate I always felt that I had a strong responsibility to nurture them through that after a show opened.

Yes. Even if something does well critically, it can feel reductive after everybody's put so much care and time and creative energy into something to have one review be the thing that makes everyone view it as successful or not. And that can be hard, especially on young writers. I think somebody who's been through it a number of times realizes it's okay, your career continues and life continues and you have to take the good with the bad. Sometimes it really is just one person's opinion. But it happens to be one that has a lot of weight and influence.

We've talked a lot about your relationship with writers. Can you tell me more about your relationship with directors and the rest of the creative team? How do you match a writer up to a director? And when a creative team is working on a show, how do you see your role in relation to the production?

At LCT3, I was very hands-on because there were only myself and my associate, Natasha, who were focused on the work there. I was involved from beginning to end in a very hands-on way with all of the shows. Here, we have a bigger staff, and I have many other responsibilities – a lot more fundraising. So I'm less hands-on with the individual productions. But I'm still involved, and when it's a new play I'm quite involved in its development. I come from being a dramaturge, so I work on developing the play with the director and the writer.

In terms of pairing the director and the writer, that landscape has changed in the time that I've been working in theatre. It used to be that plays would come to a theatre unattached. Now, oftentimes, they're already 'packaged' by the agency where the writer is represented, paired with a director at that agency. At LCT3, for maybe 40 or 50 per cent of the plays, I paired a director with the writer. But some of the plays came with a director who'd been working on it for quite some time. Before I'll hire any director, I have to see their work because that's the only way to know how they direct. I'm loath to separate a collaboration unless I've seen a director's work and I think it's really not strong. Otherwise, I'll honour the collaboration and honour the fact that they've been working together.

When I'm matching a director and a playwright, I'll ask two or three directors to read the play and then have them talk with the playwright. I talk with the directors and the playwright talks with the directors, and almost always we agree on who is the best choice. It's the same with designers. Usually I want to honour whomever the director wants to work with – if they've collaborated before it helps, but I won't say yes to designers unless I think their work is good.

One of the great things about new writing in New York is that writers come from a real range backgrounds in terms of culture, ethnicity, gender and sexuality and so on. Are there any voices or communities that you feel are not being represented at the moment? Where do you think that conversation about diversity should go?

We can do better with diversifying both on stage and with community outreach. How do you make people who aren't generally theatre-goers into theatre-goers? And how do you let them know that there are $30 tickets available? Social media and online marketing are helpful because you can target specific zip codes and do targeted outreach. But it's a big challenge. How do you address the greying of the audience? How do you diversify the audience ethnically, generationally, socio-economically and so on?

A new thing we're doing next season is education matinees with public school kids. Stephen Adly Guirgis felt strongly about that. He started out working with at-risk youth and he wanted education matinees for his shows where he'll talk with the high school students at talkbacks, do playwriting workshops and so on. That will be new for Signature, and I think it will be a great way of helping to diversify the audiences.

And who are the artistic voices that you'd like to hear more from? I don't mean individuals but rather, which groups, people or communities would you like to feature more on stage in the long term?

Given what's going on in this country at the moment, it seems like voices of people who are immigrants would be important. For Signature that's harder to do because we commit to a body of work rather than to one production. But I certainly want the writers who we bring here for residencies to be an eclectic, diverse group with many different points of view.

Well, with Trump and Brexit, we are living through a very particular political moment, aren't we? Do you think that either theatre as a form or the theatre that you run has a role to play in that kind of political environment?

I think that's up to the individual artistic director. Work that is directly of-the-moment is often less interesting to me artistically. I hope that work will live beyond its moment. The artistry of it is important to me – I'm not really interested in agitprop. In any commissioning or developmental process, I think it's best for writers to write about something that's driving them and that feels organic to whatever they're thinking about, though I imagine that the current political situation in the United States will work its way into a lot of writers' plays.

I would agree that the chances of a play which simply says: 'Donald Trump's a bad guy' being any good are low. But inevitably, politics is likely to be implicit in the work of any writer who is drawn to people on the margins or who represents communities that are marginalized by the 'mainstream' – even if they're not directly addressing specific issues.

Yes. That's certainly true of Stephen Adly Giurgis, Lynn Nottage and Dominique Morisseau. But oftentimes a good writer will come at something from an angle that feels like it will resonate beyond the exact moment or situation that the writer is responding to.

Who are the artistic directors who have been particularly influential on you?

Lynne Meadow and André Bishop because I learned from them and came up under them. I wouldn't say there's anyone where I think: 'I want to do exactly what that person's doing.' So much of it is instinct, and I want always to trust my own instincts because if you lose that then it's very hard to do the job well. I admire what Oskar Eustis has done at The Public. There's some very exciting work going on there and he has expanded the programming a lot. Sarah Benson is doing unique and very strong work at Soho Rep. I've learned from many different people just by watching what they do. Ultimately, I think you have to trust your instincts in any kind of job where there's an artistic element because if you start second-guessing yourself then it's very hard to do the job.

5
ROBERT FALLS

Robert Falls was artistic director of Wisdom Bridge Theatre, Chicago, from 1977 to 1985 where he produced a mixed programme of new and classic plays. He has been artistic director of the Goodman Theatre in Chicago since 1985. One of the oldest theatres in the United States, the Goodman has two performance spaces, a 750-seat mainhouse and a smaller studio theatre.

Could you tell me about your journey to becoming artistic director at the Goodman?

I'm a bit unusual compared to most American artistic directors in that I've never done anything else except be an artistic director and a director at the same time. I have had exactly forty straight years of running two different theatre companies. I'm simultaneously extraordinarily proud of that and embarrassed by it – because it seems an obscene amount of time to be running theatres! But yet that's how my life has worked out.

I grew up in downstate Illinois. I went to high school in the Chicago area and then went directly from there to the University of Illinois. So my entire experience has been in the Midwest. By the mid-1970s, I was in my early twenties and I arrived in Chicago as an actor. And very quickly, really within about a year and a half of working here, I came into contact with a very, very small company called Wisdom Bridge Theatre, which had about 150 seats. It was 1977 and the founding artistic director of that company became ill and had to leave. There was a small ensemble of five actors who had been with him since the founding of the company in 1974 and they asked me if I would take over. This all sounds very glamorous, of course, but it meant that alongside directing three out of five productions a year there, I would have to roll in first thing in the morning and clean the toilets and pick up the programmes and open the box office, and essentially, with two other people, run an entire theatre company, with a very small amount of money. Nowadays, since I've been running one of the largest theatres in the country for thirty years, it's easy to forget that my roots really were that simple. But I remain connected to the hundreds of small theatres in Chicago that operate in exactly the same way, to this day.

But Wisdom Bridge gave me an opportunity to direct while also learning how to be an artistic director from the ground up. I had to learn how to create a small institution, so I brought in people who knew how to do this far better than I did. I had to establish a board of trustees, which meant finding people who actually believed there had to be a reason for the Wisdom Bridge Theatre to exist in the neighbourhood we were in.

Whereabouts was it?

It was on Howard Street which is the last street in the city of Chicago, going north, and was a very rough and tumble, working-class neighbourhood with a long, seedy history. There wasn't anything up there except this small theatre of 150 seats, above a seedy bar and rather elegant violin shop. So very quickly I had to identify and work with people who believed in the work that we were doing, which was essentially a combination of new plays and revivals of off-Broadway successes – productions that had already tested their mettle somewhere else. The second thing that we had to do, which was essential, and remains essential but complicated forty years later, was to create a subscription audience. This was a new thing at the time. There was a remarkable man named Danny Newman who had transformed Chicago's Lyric Opera and many other American theatres, having created the concept of subscription. This was the idea of encouraging people to commit to a season of work, rather than just individual plays. He wrote a book in the mid-1970s called *Subscribe Now*, which is the bible of building an audience. And Wisdom Bridge was at the forefront of this among small theatres in Chicago. But it worked and we were able to build an audience, which meant that, financially, we knew at the beginning of the year, how much money we had. We built a knowledgeable, deep-pocketed group of people who supported the work that we were doing. Eventually I was able to bring in a partner as a producorial director to take over the producorial side of things that I had no particular talent for. And even though Wisdom Bridge was small, we really achieved both national and international success, including touring some of our productions to Great Britain – we ended up at the Lyric, Hammersmith for an extended run.

And then you took over at the Goodman. Obviously you've been there a long time now, but when you started, did you feel the history of that place was shaping the way that you thought and programmed? And how did you seek to shift that organization and change it into your own image?

Well, I don't think it radically shifted. The Goodman has an extremely long history – it's the second oldest resident theatre in the United States after the Cleveland Playhouse, which was founded somewhere around 1915. But the Goodman was founded in 1925 and it has a long and complex history both as a professional theatre but also as an academic theatre with students. It was connected to a training programme that was very famous for a long period of time. And there was a period when all of the directors working here were European, and then it had lots of directors who had established commercial careers in New York City and so on. But my predecessor, Gregory Mosher, was very young when he took over – in his late twenties. And he and Roche Schulfer (who was the executive director then and still is now) saw it into a new era. They were rather aligned with the work of David Mamet, who was the resident writer at that time, and they changed the tone of the Goodman Theatre to focus on younger work, new playwrights and innovative productions of classic material with interesting directors. The theatre had been a bit dusty and musty for the twenty years prior to that. But suddenly you've got this director and managing director in their late twenties that changed all that.

So when I was brought in, it wasn't like I had to come and utterly change everything. But there was one key shift. Gregory, as a director, was far more interested in intimate work on a very small stage. And at that time the Goodman had a 120-seat theatre, but also it had main house of about 750 seats or thereabouts. And in my small 150-seat theatre at Wisdom Bridge, I had been doing productions of *Hamlet*, *The Tempest*, *Mother Courage and Her Children* and so on. So when I got to the Goodman, I was interested in revitalizing the larger theatre. Because I felt like it had been operating like the other small theatres in town.

Chicago feels like a very specific place to be making work. The theatre culture there is very different from London or New York.
That is exactly true. There is this cliché of Chicago being an ensemble town – an actor-driven town, and that's true. It has a rawer, rougher, no bullshit mid-Western aesthetic.

It's interesting you say that. I was speaking to somebody who ran one of the ensembles in Chicago, and he was talking about the difference between New York actors and Chicago actors. He said that Chicago actors are much more blue collar than they are in New York. Would you agree with that?
Yes. In fact, there was a point in time where many of the most prominent actors around were not only blue collar, they were either ex-police officers or they were ex-criminals. These were not people who went to drama school! Of course, a lot of the companies that formed in Chicago were modelled very specifically on the Steppenwolf Theatre ensemble, which was a group of actors who had all gone to university together, had then moved to the nearest big city and had developed an ensemble style. And forty years later, that remains a magnet that draws young theatre companies to the city.

What I wanted to do was harness the energy of that rough and tumble acting community, towards plays by Shakespeare, by Ibsen, by Moliere. Of course, we still produced an unusual amount of new plays, but it was that large-scale work, those big classic productions, that made the Goodman different.

When you're programming, what draws you to an individual project or to an individual artist? And how do you go about curating an overall season?
At Wisdom Bridge, I would essentially programme five play seasons and I'd choose plays that balanced each other in an interesting way. Then I would direct three of them and hire two people to direct the others. That was a standard model at the time and, essentially, it remains standard today. But I began to get tired of that. And at around the time I was offered the Goodman Theatre, I also received a grant that

enabled me to travel to Great Britain. I was interested in different models of theatres, especially those that were director driven as opposed to the ensemble led. So I ended up spending some time at the Royal Shakespeare Company when Trevor Nunn was running it. At the time he had a number of associate directors working alongside him. And I was fascinated by the fact that there was this group of four or five different directors who all had a common goal of reinvigorating Shakespeare.

I also spent some highly influential time in Glasgow at the Citizens Theatre. I was fascinated by the fact that it was run by a triumvirate of Giles Havergall who was a director and actor; Phillip Prowse who was a director, designer and actor; and Robert David MacDonald who was a playwright and director. They were running a theatre in a working-class neighbourhood and making rather highfalutin classical work for low prices. So what I did when I started at the Goodman was to bring in two other very strong Chicago-based directors so I wouldn't be alone with only my own ideas.

Who were the people you brought in?
One was a brilliant director who is sadly no longer with us – a man named Michael Maggio. The other was a really seminal director, called Frank Galati. He was also an educator at Northwestern University and influenced an enormous generation of directors including Mary Zimmerman, for example. And both Frank and Mike had very different aesthetics from me.

Now obviously there is a big question of diversity here. At that time, the mid-1980s, having three white men running a theatre was not uncommon. But over the years, probably the biggest single thing that happened to me is my realization of the responsibility I have to the diversity and complexity of the city of Chicago.

Well, there's a very strong racial divide in Chicago, isn't there?
Yes, the segregation of the city of Chicago has always been neighbourhood-oriented.

That's what Bruce Norris' play *Clybourne Park* is about isn't it?
Yes. Chicago can be very divided and divisive. But it is also a city of extraordinary vitality because of those different communities. Of course, every city has its own complexity, but I've always said that

Chicago has both the best of the United States and the worst of the United States. So diversity became increasingly important for me. And over the years I have increased the cultural, ethnic, racial and even aesthetic diversity of our artistic collective. For instance, it was very clear that African Americans needed to be essential to our mission. There's been a long, rich history of African American work coming out of the neighbourhoods of Chicago. And I was a great admirer of the remarkable Chuck Smith, who became an early associate about twenty years ago and is an advocate for African American writers and classic black work. There is a wonderful director named Henry Godinez, who is a Cuban American and was very active running a Latino Theatre Company in the early 1980s, and he came in with a similar sort of the mission.

So I would have conversations with that artistic collective about what plays they wanted to do over a three- or four-year period. These might be classic plays or musical works that were going to take a while to develop, and it could involve identifying and advocating for emerging or younger directors to work with. I often use a gardening metaphor – it's like we plant seeds early on and ultimately harvest the fruit when it's ready. And that is not always easy – it meant people were not necessarily guaranteed a play within any particular season, but they would end up with something within a two- or three-year period. And this sort of changed the face of the Goodman because it gave the audience a relationship to the directors. It demonstrated that it was directors' vision that was guiding the institution.

So your process was led by gathering this informal group of associates, ensuring they're diverse gender-wise and ethnically and giving them each an opportunity, with your guidance, to create several shows?

That's right. They all have a real voice and they all also have a financial relationship to the theatre. But it varies from individual to individual. Some people are very interested in being involved with the running of the theatre in a wider sense, and then there are others who have no interest in that whatsoever. And this system also allows people to go around the country doing other work. But hopefully, when they have their most interesting ideas, or the ideas that may need the most resources, they can look to the Goodman as a sort of base.

But just to go back to diversity for a moment, an early model of mine, in this regard, was Joe Papp. He was such a major figure for any artistic director in the United States. And for my generation and me he was a great leader in terms of cultural diversity when it came to casting. I hate that phrase 'colour-blind casting' because I am not colour-blind and I do think that if you are looking to develop parity when it comes to the work of women in the theatre, or to the work of people of colour then, at least in my case, I had to develop that very consciously.

Sue Emmas, who is the associate artistic director at the Young Vic in London, says that she doesn't like the term 'colour-blind'; she prefers the phrase 'colour-conscious'. It seems to me that the problem with the idea of colour-blindness is that it implies that we shouldn't see colour on stage because we shouldn't see it in life, but that ignores the fact that things like colour continue to play a massive role in our society and so you have to reflect those tensions and dynamics in the work – even if your intention, ultimately, is to subvert them.

Absolutely. And fairly early on, the Goodman became a leader when it came to diverse casting in its productions. Of course, I will still respect it if a director says: 'Well, I'm directing Arthur Miller's *Death of a Salesman*, which is a play about a family and it would be somewhat distracting if they didn't look like they were related.' But there's no reason, if you're doing Shakespeare or Ibsen or Chekhov and so on that you shouldn't cast diversely. But we're also led by playwrights. The great August Wilson was a very important writer to the Goodman Theatre. We premiered two of his ten plays and we were the first theatre in the United States to do the whole Pittsburgh Cycle. And he's an example of a major artist who didn't really want to see cultural or colour diversity in the casting of his plays.

It's interesting for me to look at what is happening in England, and in London in particular, which has become extremely conscious of diversity after a long history of not being so. Certainly the number of women running major institutions there has really increased whereas that is still a problem in this country. The search for parity, here, in terms of the number of plays by women that are produced and the number of women that are directing, is something we have to continue.

It is true that there has been a significant increase in the number of prominent venues in the UK that are run by women. But nationally, it is still the case that less than a third of directors working in major theatres are women. So the prominence of female leadership in the big shiny venues might still be masking a deeper problem. And there is a great degree of ethnic diversity on the London stage at the moment, but I have artist friends of colour who remain sceptical and say: 'Yeah, give it five years and let's see if that's still the case.' So it feels like there is still work to do and we shouldn't be complacent.

Yes, though I find it a little difficult to believe that we will go backwards. Over the past twenty years, even under the Bush Administration, there has still been a progressive openness within the arts. Progress may be slow, but then again, I would not have thought gay marriage would have happened as fast as it did – considering what resistance there was to it in the United States for such a long period of time. So you hope that that could happen with other similar things. So I think that political events now are a call to arms for the arts that will accelerate our political work and will drive a movement, which is progressive and necessary at a time when things have been dismantled on so many other levels.

Could you say something about the relationship between Chicago and New York in theatrical terms? Is there a tension that exists between the two or is there a healthy relationship?

I don't think Chicago thinks about it all that often honestly. I don't think the shadow of New York hovers over us at all. With Chicago actors, playwrights and directors there is just a sense getting on with the job. One of the reasons that Chicago theatre grew is that the rents were cheaper and the beers were cheaper. And so actors go about doing their work with no expectations of stardom. They commit to an ensemble, they commit to their work, they go to their show, the drink afterwards, and they fuck each other – which is the same thing that happens with theatre everywhere.

But then, when the production opens, whether it's a success and the critics like it, or it fails and the critics and audiences don't like it, it doesn't really affect them. They will still get up the next morning and continue to go about their work. Whereas in New York success or failure can have a far more positive or negative effect: you can become a superstar quickly or crash and burn quickly. Someone once said to me that for playwrights in New York, there is a sort of three strikes and 'you're out' mentality. You get three opportunities and if you're not successful, that could really affect your career because New York does remain driven by a ruthless commercialism – which also now exists off-Broadway. And I don't think that's a very healthy environment for making work.

Finally, who are the artistic directors whom you most admire?

That's a great question – you know directors are notoriously difficult when it comes to crediting anyone else with any success! There are many of my colleagues whom I admire tremendously: Oskar Eustis at The Public Theater for instance or Diane Paulus for the work that she's done at the A.R.T. But it's interesting because I think I still remain influenced by the people I looked up to when I was young. People like Gordon Davidson at Center Theatre Group in Los Angeles or Zelda Fichandler at Arena Stage in DC – these are people who were founders of their theatre companies. To be honest, anybody who brings success or brings personality to their theatre company will be someone whom I admire tremendously.

6

VICKY FEATHERSTONE

Vicky Featherstone was artistic director of the new writing touring company Paines Plough from 1997 to 2004. She was then the founding artistic director of the National Theatre of Scotland (NTS), a non-building-based company, which she ran until 2012 when she was appointed artistic director of the Royal Court. Based in Chelsea, London, the Royal Court produces new plays in both its 380-seat main space and its 85-seat studio space.

Tell me about your journey through all of the companies you have run.

The first building I had a long-term relationship with was the West Yorkshire Playhouse through the Regional Theatre Young Director Scheme in 1991–1992. Jude Kelly was artistic director and I was there for two years as assistant director. That was my first understanding of what an artistic director could do. She was an amazing role model because I saw the potential of that role – it wasn't just about making art but also about shaping the context in which that art is made. That really excited me because my background, in terms of how I had learnt about theatre at Manchester University, was quite a politicized one. So for me, the context around how we communicate with audiences and who we're bringing in to the theatre is always as important as the actual art itself. And that isn't the case for a lot of people.

I then went on to work at Bolton Octagon and at Northern Stage. But I gradually realized that what I really wanted to concentrate on was new writing. So I decided to move to London because there wasn't really a new writing scene happening outside the capital. When I arrived here I wrote about 200 letters to people asking for work. I had a CV of loads of things I'd directed outside of London, but because no one had seen it no one cared. I had a meeting with Dominic Dromgoole at the Bush and he said: 'I don't care that you've directed a show at the West Yorkshire Playhouse or Northern Stage. People haven't seen it so you'll never get a job.' He was brutally honest! But then, the Bush needed a literary associate for the summer, so I ended up doing that alongside Sarah Kane who was also there at the time. This was when *Blasted* was on at the Court and I thought to myself: 'This is exactly the world I want to be in.'

Eventually, Dominic took a risk on me and let me direct a show. But, of course, it's really very hard to build a freelance career. I directed a few things, but I ended up getting a proper job and working in television as a script editor. It was well paid, but I felt really defeated because it wasn't pure in the way I believed theatre could be.

Then the Paines Plough job came up. I went out for a drink one night with my friend Phelim McDermott who runs Improbable Theatre and he said I should apply. Initially I didn't want to because the company had a lot of problems. But he really challenged me. He said: 'You've got to stop going on about being unhappy in television if you're not going to go for an opportunity like this!' So I thought: 'I'll apply for it and if I get it, that's amazing. If not, I'll just commit to what is starting to be a really good career in television.' And I got the job. I was twenty-seven and basically, I've been an artistic director ever since, without even a week's break, and I'm fifty now!

Your focus on both the art and the context is really interesting. How different have the contexts felt from Paines Plough to NTS to the Royal Court?

Well, in terms of focusing on the purity of the artist – their voice and what they need to say – it is the same. At Paines Plough and the Royal Court that artist is always the playwright. At NTS it was different because the primary creators were more variable – they could be a choreographer or a director or someone else. But my role in all of those contexts is to protect the purity of that artist's vision and to support them to deliver their potential. In some ways I actually felt that Paines Plough and NTS were quite similar. Although Paines Plough happens to be based in London, at its best it's a company that is really nationally focused. It's about trying to create meaningful relationships that develop writers outside London and build audiences outside London. So the context of those two companies was similar in terms of feeling that the whole country should have ownership over the work.

When I first went for the NTS job, I had a really interesting discussion with David Greig[1] about: 'What would success look like for a National theatre in Scotland?' We felt that within the first three to four years it didn't mean that everyone had to have seen the work. Rather, it might be enough that somebody's grandchild had done an NTS workshop in school or something like that. You start thinking about context and about what ownership means in a much more multilayered way. It's not always about people buying tickets. It's about connection and reach and all those things.

So it's about people feeling that the company is present in their lives even if they haven't directly engaged with it themselves?

Exactly. That really informed the layered model we created for the company. We realized that, on the one hand, we needed to come up with big popular shows that could fill those large 2,000-seat theatres that would be glorious and celebratory of that Scottish culture of variety and pantomime; while on the other hand, we should be making work in the context of the much edgier Glasgow School of Arts world, which may get a much smaller audience but would encourage some really exciting artists to work with us. And as well as that we had a massive touring strategy.

Then, coming to the Royal Court was a huge gearshift. I've always been obsessed with playwrights so this was somewhere I'd wanted to work for such a long time. But I'd stopped wishing for it because it felt so rarified and I'd never got a job here as a freelancer. You see, I'm a really optimistic person. I cannot live my life in disappointment. I'm one of those people who think: 'If they don't want me, then fuck it. I don't care. I'm going to do something else,' rather than going 'Oh my God, I haven't been accepted into that small elite enclave.' I think that comes from having been at Manchester University – I'm just like: 'Fuck them, if I'm not part of it!'

When I arrived back in London in 2013, I felt like a lot had changed in the ten years that I'd been away. Theatre had become truly successful

[1]Scottish playwright. Artistic director of the Lyceum Theatre in Edinburgh since 2016.

in that time and it had become much more competitive as a result. I was really shocked because I'd never had to exist in such a highly competitive world in the same way before and that made me really question my instinct – in the past I'd always been able to follow my instincts. But it was quite a challenge having donors say: 'Well, I prefer what's happening at the Donmar or the Almeida, so I'm going to give my money to them.' I was really naive. I thought it would just be about: who were the writers whom we should develop and what should we put on? But it wasn't like that.

How did you deal with that?

I understood it very quickly. But I resented it because I felt it wasn't about the purity of mission for each individual theatre. This competitiveness in London meant we were a part of a huge success culture, but that didn't make what we were doing, individually, any easier or any better. Some people weren't prepared to give you a chance unless you had a hit like *The Ferryman*[2] immediately.

And that made me really question what this theatre is for. I was thinking: 'It's been here for sixty years. When has the Royal Court been at its absolute best?' And it's not actually the hit shows. The Court is at its best when it's found writers and enabled them to write things that change the way other writers write. So whenever I leave here, and I look back on that legacy, of course, I want to have had some hit shows because that keeps people coming in. But actually the legacy needs to be about how we have changed the way people write.

I have a similar feeling when people ask me which show I was proudest of at the Gate. My response is that the thing I am proudest of isn't a show – it's watching young directors I've championed go on to flourish elsewhere. Whether that is Caroline Byrne directing *Twelfth Night* at the Globe, or Jude Christian doing *Lela and Co* here at the Court. I've invested in those two directors enormously and it is thrilling to see them fly.

I understand that completely. For me one of the things I am proudest of was a play called *The Drowned World* by Gary Owen that we did at

---

[2]Play by Jez Butterworth. It won both the Evening Standard and Olivier Awards for Best New Play.

Paines Plough. It only had a small run, but so many writers and directors have told me that it inspired them.

Obviously you've had a big shift from running companies without buildings like Paines Plough and NTS to here, where you're surrounded by bricks and mortar. How has that affected the way you make work?
I love the sense of people being made to feel at home here. I love that a building is able to truly create a sense of warmth. On the other hand, there are huge limitations. If somebody came to us at NTS with a project, we could find exactly the right form – literally in terms of the space and everything – to make it. And you could actually take a show *to* the right audience. Whereas here, we are always filling the same slot effectively. Sometimes I get frustrated when people bring us work and I think: 'My God if I was at NTS, that piece of work would be extraordinary. You could do it along the Embankment or something like that.' 'Whereas, because we're the Royal Court, people will look at it through a specific lens and, as a play, it's not going to work. And it's hard because we have so few slots in a year compared to the amount of people that I would like to work with. So every time we make an announcement, rather than feeling pride for the things we're doing, I feel sadness for the things we're not doing.

The Royal Court has such an extraordinary history – whereas NTS obviously didn't have any history because you founded it. Does that history ever feel like a burden or is it something you can stand on top of?
I've never felt that it's a burden. In fact, I think my experiences in Scotland really set me up to be able to do this job. The political responsibility of setting up a national theatre and the financial responsibility of making that work were huge. Going to a country as an outsider and starting something from zero was scary. So comparatively, coming here wasn't as intimidating as I think it might have been. I'd assisted here once before, but otherwise I'd never worked here. So I came in thinking: 'The Royal Court has always felt too closed and too elite so I'm just going to be really different.' I didn't feel the burden of past directors, which I think other people have really felt because they've been much more closely

connected to the world here. My feeling was only the joy of past writers whom I've always wanted to work with and direct, so it felt very free.

How do you begin a relationship with a writer? And how does the commissioning and producing process work?

Obviously it's different for each writer. When I was at Paines Plough, I read a script by a then little-known writer called Dennis Kelly and we invited him to meet with myself and Lucy Morrison and we got on brilliantly. So we said we'd like him to come and be a resident playwright. And he said: 'What does that mean?' And I said: 'I don't know, but I think it just means you coming in and sitting on a sofa and having lots of chats.' So for me it's about relationships rather than that very London thing of being product based or success based. It's about really creating an emotional space to have conversations, to find connections and to talk about the world. The most productive relationships are the ones where that can happen.

Nowadays it's slightly different because I can't personally have that many of those great big old-school organic relationships that I've had with people like Dennis Kelly, Gary Owen, Jack Thorne and Abi Morgan. But what's exciting is that we have such a fantastic artistic planning team that I can make sure that somebody has got that relationship with each writer. You have to allow those conversations to meander and to just find what they need to be. Creating that space for meandering is really, really important as well as saying 'Here's a commission and we want to put your play on.'

How do you then put together a season? Do you just programme what is ready or do you work to a theme?

Sometimes it's pragmatically about what's ready. At other times it's about having this incredible idea or thing and then pushing for it to be ready because it's important right now. And we have to take a risk on it being ready for that to happen. And even if it is not 'themed' I need to feel like the work is having a conversation with itself.

Programming always starts off feeling like you've got a whole box of Quality Street where you have a lot of things to choose from. But then panic sets in when you get to the point of having to make final decisions and you end up losing a lot of your favourite things. So it's a mixture of feeling like you have the biggest sweetie jar in the world and then thinking: 'Fuck, it's not going to work.' You feel both joyful and paranoid at the same time.

You've talked about the politics that you imbibed in Manchester and the way that has driven you and your work, and you've talked about context a lot. Obviously, the Royal Court is located in Sloane Square, one of the richest places in the world. So how do you square that context with your politics and with your desire to make work that reaches out as far as possible?
Initially, I thought that if you were to start the Royal Court now you wouldn't start it here. You'd start it in an area that you felt was in sympathy with what you believe politically. But then I thought actually that's too obvious. In its past the Court has been described as being 'oppositional', so, in fact, this is exactly where we should be! I mean I would never, ever come to Chelsea if it wasn't for the fact that my job is here. I'm deeply middle class but I would never see this much affluence normally. And so this context is really useful for me, oddly.

But also the fundamental context for this theatre has to be about the writer, so actually we could be based anywhere. And as long as we're having the biggest conversations with writers both from Britain and internationally, then that's what's really important.

In relation to this question of politics and context, the theatre industry is currently dominated by the conversation around the issues of diversity and inclusion. What do those terms mean to you?
I think we're at different stages with the different groups that we are trying to be representative of. For instance, I never think about gender in relation to diversity. I haven't had to for years because I've never not had a gender-balanced programme. More generally, we're in a much better place than we were. When I came back to London after ten years away in Scotland, which is essentially quite a white country, I was really thrilled to have the opportunity to work in a more diverse way. So I was quite shocked to discover that it felt like less was happening here than when I had left. And I rang up Kwame Kwei-Armah to talk to him about this and he said: 'Well, it's because everyone got bored of it.' But in the last four years, that has changed dramatically.

I also think dramatic structure is really important in this conversation. As long as we focus on the structure of the 'well-made play' then we're not going to be discomforted by different voices. Because a conventional structure makes us feel comfortable and so the content isn't ever going to be really radical. Content can be illuminating, of course, but form is the only really radical thing. If we are familiar with a structure, it gives us sense of safety because we know that everything is either going to be alright at the end or it's not. And we know how to handle both of those things. So we're never going to be shifted in a new way. I think what's interesting here is that we haven't enabled or encouraged a diverse middle-class voice. What we've encouraged is a more – and I hate this word, but the Royal Court used to use it a lot – 'authentic voice'. And so sadly that work is often peripheral because our inability to be judgemental of it means that we are often not that rigorous with what the structure is. So consequently we're not necessarily helping those artists move into the centre because we're not being rigorous with them.

But in terms of other groups – Jenny Sealey of Graeae always talks about how disability is still such a taboo in theatre. It's really exciting when theatre is made with disabled artists at the centre as primary creators because you come up with thrilling new forms for how theatre can feel and look – that is something that's so brilliant about her work. work, though that's quite challenging with the Royal Court because we're writer led. When I was in Scotland, I was able to work with some disabled artists and I felt really proud of the work that we made. Because they were primary creators, you didn't worry about whether it was movement, dance, theatre or whatever – it was just the thing that was made. Whereas here, we still start from asking what the play will look like on the page. So the Court is still very behind in that regard, though I think we are better in terms of ethnic diversity.

You clearly have a real taste for formally inventive work, but you have still programmed a lot of shows here that are more conventionally structured. Would you, in an ideal world, not do those conventional plays? Or do you still think they have value?
I think they have real value because I love a story and so I absolutely love those plays. I think it's really important that those brilliant playwrights feel that we really care about them and that this is a home for them. If

any writer says: 'They wouldn't be interested in the way I write,' then I'm not doing my job properly. Those more conventional, character-led, well-made plays with big themes are really important.

Who are the artistic directors who have inspired you?

I think that when Nick Hytner took over at the National, even though a lot of the work wasn't necessarily to my taste, he made a massive shift that isn't actually properly acknowledged. And obviously, as it went on there were issues like there were not enough women playwrights and so on. But actually the change that happened from it being a sort of old-school theatre into something which felt like it was beginning to have different conversations was probably one of the greatest that we've seen. So that was an incredibly important artistic directorship.

And then you look at people like Philip Hedley when he was running Theatre Royal Stratford East. He did extraordinary things bringing in so many artists and starting so many conversations, and Kerry Michael has carried on doing that even though that venue is often forgotten in terms of the wider London picture. And there are so many of my peers who are doing such incredible things like Tom Morris in Bristol, Roxana Silbert in Birmingham and Gemma Bodinetz in Liverpool. I also feel that what Rupert Goold did at Headlong was incredible – he was fearless about what touring should mean and the kind of work that you should make.

But the other person whom I think is unbelievable is David Greig at the Lyceum. He's got one of the most magnificent theatre brains of anyone I've ever known. And I think you understand the narrative behind every one of his choices – it's oozing with the mission! So at the moment I would say that he's the most inspirational artistic director to me. What he's doing is incredible against a lot of difficult odds. So I hope he can stay that ambitious and keep wearing his beliefs on his sleeve in that way.

7
SARAH FRANKCOM

Sarah Frankcom was associate artistic director and then joint artistic director at the Royal Exchange, Manchester, from 2008 until 2014 when she took over as sole artistic director. The Exchange is a 700-seat theatre in the round in the heart of Manchester. It also has a smaller studio space.

Could you tell me about your journey to becoming artistic director of Manchester Royal Exchange?
It was a big accident really. I never imagined that I'd be an artistic director – there's been no plan at all! When I was young, I was part of a really brilliant youth theatre in Sheffield and through that I realized that I wanted to be a drama teacher. So after university, I did a PGCE in London that got me really interested in theatre and education: working in prisons, making work with non-professionals and so on. I did that for about seven or eight years. Through that, I encountered various actors and a playwright, and we started to make work that could be used to tour schools and deliver on the curriculum. Then, by complete accident, one of the first shows we made, a new play by a woman called Nicola Baldwin, got picked up and had a run on the fringe and went on to win the George Devine Award. Someone from the National Theatre came to see that, and so I ended up at the National Theatre Studio. The Studio worked in a really weird way back then, where you didn't quite know why you'd been invited in and you didn't quite know what was expected of you. But they just let us carry on developing and experimenting and we then made our next show, which they invested in.

So I started to make more work on the fringe and I became increasingly involved in new writing. But by the age of thirty, I thought to myself: 'I can't afford to do this anymore.' I wasn't getting anywhere with people wanting to give me work as a director, so I thought: 'I want to work in a building, and so I'll use what I think I'm good at, which is education, and see if I can get a job in an education department.' But I singularly failed to be able to do that.

Then, on a complete off-chance, I applied to be the literary manager at the Royal Exchange, and to my absolute surprise, I got the job. This was back in 2000. It was a really interesting time to come here because the theatre had just had a big refurbishment. So there was a new studio space where I could develop and commission writers. But at that point, I don't think I ever thought I was going to be here for very long. And I certainly didn't give myself permission to think I might be involved in the artistic leadership of a place like this.

When that job came to an end, I went off to be a freelancer but I was eventually asked back to the Exchange as the associate artistic director. So I guess my career has been unusual because I've essentially had a very long apprenticeship in one building. Then, about three years ago, having spent several years working alongside Greg Hersov and Braham Murray, I took over as the sole artistic director when the old regime dismantled itself. It's interesting, previously this building had always been run by a group of directors. It had never had a solo artistic director before.

How has that change affected the building?
When it was run by a group there were not only some real positives but also some real negatives. It meant that a small group of people were making an awful lot of work here, and because that group of people shared the same taste essentially, that determined a lot of the artistic choices in this building over a number of decades.

Did that make it feel quite insular?
Well, in its DNA, this building has always been kind of a maverick – it has pursued its own agenda. It's always believed in creating work that responds to the democracy of the space. And it's always believed in cultivating the relationship between the old and the new. Going right back to the foundation of the company in 1976, there's been a strong dialogue that has come from the fact that for every old play we do, we invest in a new one. And that has meant we've always had a very

healthy audience for new work. It's great to be in a building where you can commission playwrights and encourage them to take on a 700-seat space and know that if the play is good, then the company would take the risk and programme it and you could be pretty confident that 10,000 people would come and see it. It is really unusual in this country for that to happen.

But did it feel insular? Yes, it could be very insular. And, for me, what that meant was that this building just moved at its own pace and didn't really respond to changes in the outside world. This was especially true in relation to the city itself. Manchester, over that period of time, absolutely transformed itself. It's developed a huge confidence culturally, and there is an ambition and outward-looking internationalism that has allowed other cultural organizations here to really set their sights on being world leaders. But I think the Exchange didn't really do that. Nobody here really noticed that that was going on outside and I found that quite frustrating.

So when I took over solo, we went through a process where I was asked to reframe and rearticulate a vision for the building. I described what I wanted to do as opening the doors and letting a new energy in. This building has a hugely loyal audience, but we actually needed to turn our attention to look, very seriously, at the vast parts of our community that simply don't engage with us or with our art form. There was also a very culturally literate audience that wouldn't necessarily think about coming here because it seemed quite moribund – the kind of theatre that their parents would come to.

I guess my perspective has been very shaped by the fact that my first experience of going to the theatre was as a participant in a learning project. I don't really come from the kind of background where I would have felt readily at home and comfortable in a cultural building. So making really high-quality participation opportunities available and accessible to the widest variety of people has always been critical for me.

Also, when I took over, there was a big debate in which people were questioning the value of theatre buildings. After all, they have a lot of staff so they're very expensive to run. They gobble up money, which could be going directly to artists. We get 2 million pounds of Arts Council subsidy and we do attract a quite significant audience, but pound for pound, there's probably a cheaper model for putting work out there for audiences. But, for me, the best argument that you can make in defence of a building is that people know where you are and you don't move. And that is critical in terms of access. That said, we've got a very long way to go before we can truly say that we are a local theatre that's open and available and an essential part of everybody's life in Manchester.

What's the road map for that journey?

There are two starting points. The first has to do with our community work. Partly, this has involved growing the young company – so now it is about four, five times the size that it was. And we are diversifying the people that we're making it available to. We're also trying to use it as a training ground where we can introduce young people to a wider variety of the elements of making theatre – we're encouraging young leaders, young technicians, young directors, young makers, young writers. And we now have quite a lot of young people who are really excited to be hanging out in our building.

Our community work has also been focused on developing a company of elders. And that actually came out of an artist-led project. In 2012, the director Max Webster made a devised piece called *My Young Foolish Heart*, which involved five young people and five older people. What was great about the show was that, for the five performances it was on, our 700-seat theatre was full and had the most diverse audience that we've ever had in the building. So we realized that there was increasingly a need for those older people to come together in the longer term. We have a director who works with them regularly and the group now has about seventy members. Our job is to really challenge them through the artists whom we invite to go in and work with them. So they've just done a wonderful piece with someone from Candoco Dance that got them moving in ways that you wouldn't have ever thought possible.

What has been really inspiring is when those two groups, the young company and the elders, have made work together. Theatre is about having conversations that can't happen in the outside world. And so it's amazing when you see young people and older people move towards a shared understanding. I believe that when you make non-professional work, you shouldn't hide it in your studio space or under-resource it; rather, you need to over-resource it. And this work genuinely feels like it has become a lived part of our mission and vision as a theatre, and I have become quite evangelical about it.

The second starting point for us had to do with audiences. We have a huge and loyal season ticket audience – between three and three-and-half thousand people. They are prepared to take a risk on us, and that's a brilliant thing. But the only relationship we have with them is through the financial transaction of them buying a ticket. So the question I asked myself was: 'Our audiences clearly have a passion for this theatre, and if we can get to understand that a bit better, might that then help us understand why some people don't engage with us? And why some people find it hard to walk up our steps? Is there a way of starting conversation with an audience that might help us think more deeply about what our programming is and does, and what it might need to be?'

So we started the *You, The Audience* programme, to learn more. And that's been quite a game changer. Because we'd been a bit insular in the past. A lot of people didn't feel empowered to tell us what they thought because they felt that we didn't really want to know. So one of the biggest barriers to overcome has been to persuade people that we really do want to know. But once you do that, some of the things that they reveal about themselves are astonishing: in terms of what they've got from the work and how the building has been a key place for people who have met their partners here and so on. Someone described how the first significant thing he did after his partner died was to come and sit in our auditorium on his own. He spoke of how he felt about that and how it was a staging post in terms of the way he went through his grief over a number of years. And because quite a lot of our team have led and been part of those conversations, people now feel that they can continue to come and talk to us. So I now know my audience in a whole new way.

How do you go about programming a season of work? What draws you to a project?

The first thing to say is that it's not just me who programmes the theatre. And this is another big area of change. Historically, programming in this building involved the artistic directors going into a room, coming up with what they wanted to do and then passing it over to people who would make it happen. But we now programme in a much more collegiate and consultative way. We have a number of projects that come through a sort of 'ideas testing' phase that involves investing money and R&D-ing stuff. And we think about what feels relevant and what we want to be asking of the world that we're living in now. And we also look at plays from the repertoire that feel most important at a given point and time.

Programming is the hardest thing an artistic director does. As anybody who runs a regional house will know, it's either boom or bust. If you're going through a good patch, doing really well at the box office, then you start to dream of doing plays with bigger cast sizes. But sometimes when you're programming, you also know that you've got a show that's crashing and that can make you risk averse. So the biggest challenge is how you keep a consistent attitude to risk-taking. It's easy to take a risk every so often, it's harder to take a risk all of the time.

I also think you really have to know what a risk is. After all, a risk for one part of our audience might actually be a really safe bet for another part of our audience. But sometimes you can get a very strong sense of the degree to which an audience will support the risk you are taking. For instance, I've had a quite long relationship with Maxine Peake over the last ten years. And while an audience won't always book in large numbers to see her, when we did *Hamlet* with her in the title role, they really supported the gesture of that production and we sold out before it opened. That, to me, is the biggest mandate that the audience or the city can give you. And every so often, when we've taken the biggest risk or what we perceived as the biggest risk, that is where the biggest reward has been.

Do you feel that you have a role as a public figure – either in Manchester specifically or in more general terms?

Yes, though I think it's the bit of my role that I've found the most difficult because I'm not naturally confident. But there is definitely a responsibility, if you're the artistic leader of a building like this, to be an advocate not only for what you're doing but for what theatre is and can be. And you have to be an advocate for other artists who don't have that kind of platform. I'm very good at rattling cages and talking about representation and diversity. I can talk about the things that I see as being problems in our sector and I can confidently advocate for artists and for talent development because we do an awful lot of that here.

In terms of advocacy within this city, I've really enjoyed engaging with other institutions in Manchester who may not fully understand who we are or what we do or what a working theatre is. That can include businesses, universities, NGOs, etc. I've enjoyed advocating for the value that theatre can have in terms of being a bridge organization between schools, housing associations and charities. We can be the place where people can meet and do things and we can break down some of the barriers that those organizations have in terms of working with each other.

One thing this building hasn't been very good at in the past is shouting about the things we do. So trying to find a way of articulating the changes we've made has been a challenge. But I think we've started to get that right. More people in the sector can see that things have moved quite a way here. That's important because often, in regional theatre, change has been seen as being synonymous with a theatre not doing very well. But a lot of the change that's happened here has come from a position of strength. We've made an active choice to change our producing model and to reconfigure some of the ways we invest in what we want to make. So we have to tell that story as loudly and as openly as we can because we're now more successful both in terms of people coming to see the work and our turnover than we've ever been.

Who are the artistic directors whom you've really looked up to?
Oskar Eustis at the Public is probably one of the greatest artistic directors. His theatre is constantly reinventing itself while still remaining true to its original mission, which is radical, relevant and inclusive – they always manage to remain slightly ahead of what our art form is and can do. When I meet artists who have worked there, they always express what an amazing building it is to be in, and I think that counts for quite a lot. It's a building that completely supports artists, and to me, that's really critical.

Also, I wouldn't be here if, as a young person, I hadn't been hanging out in a regional theatre, which was run by a female artistic director – Clare Venables at The Crucible in Sheffield. She was probably one of the only female artistic directors at the time and she was both ambitious in her programming and committed to her city. She was also very accessible and very visible – she did all her meetings in the bar.

I've also been very inspired by Madani Younis at the Bush. I think he's quite astonishing because he has been absolutely uncompromising in what he believes in and what he wants that theatre to be about. Breaking new ground can be quite lonely in the beginning. But I knew him from when he ran Freedom Studios in Bradford, and so it was very interesting seeing him arrive in London as an outsider, and going: 'I don't want to be part of the club. I just want to run the theatre.' Similarly, I'm a big fan of what Michael Buffong has done with Talawa. He reinvented that company very quickly and now it's both vital and important, which it really wasn't before. I don't think either Michael's or Madani's journeys have necessarily been that easy or straightforward, but they've made it look effortless.

And actually Nick Hytner is probably one of the best artistic directors in a certain way. There's something about how he managed to completely overhaul the National Theatre that's really impressive. I've made two shows for him. The first was in 2005 and was the premiere of Simon Stephens's play *On the Shore of the Wide World*, which was a co-production between the Exchange and the National. It had been a really difficult project, to the point where the artistic directors here had asked me to cut about a quarter of it – but neither the writer nor I thought it should be cut. Nick came to the second preview and gave me two of the best notes that I've ever had which just made all the difference. He said: 'I know they're telling you that you need to lose a part of this, but you've still got two more previews. Never ever make a big cut like that unless you truly believe in it. If you're going to go down, you might as well go down knowing that you put the work out into the world as you wanted it to be. This is the first time this play will be made. Let the next person cut it if they want to.' He was very cool, calm and to the point, and I thought that was really good advice.

So did you refuse to make the cut?

Yes. And it was the best bit of the production. One of the most critical parts of being an artistic director is understanding that what's right for one director is not necessarily right for another director. But you have a real responsibility to look after that director – and giving the right note at the right time can make or break a show sometimes. It can be really hard to tell a director that something's not working or not clear and that it needs to change. Because you're working with people when they're at their most vulnerable. But it's also thrilling. It's a great privilege to be able to be on the inside of an awful lot of different processes. I've learned a lot that way and it's challenged my own practice quite a bit. It's made me very aware that I need to make sure that I'm challenging myself as much as possible over the next projects that I make. Because it's an incredible privilege to be making a big body of work for once space.

8
KWAME KWEI-ARMAH

Kwame Kwei-Armah started out as an actor and playwright. He was artistic director of Baltimore Center Stage from 2011 to 2018. Center Stage is the state theatre of Maryland and the biggest theatre in Baltimore – its main house seats 541. In 2017, just before this interview took place, it was announced that he would take over from David Lan as artistic director of the Young Vic Theatre.

Could you tell me a little bit about your journey to becoming artistic director of Baltimore Center Stage?

I first went to Center Stage in 2004 when they produced my play *Elmina's Kitchen*. The director fell ill on the last day of rehearsals, and there was no one to take it from the rehearsal room to the stage. So I jumped in. We got it to opening night and it had gone well, and so the then artistic director, Irene Lewis, said: 'I think you could do this directing thing. Would you like to try?' I'd never really thought about directing before. But she gave me Naomi Wallace's *Things of Dry Hours* to read, and that was my first show. Now, in my humble opinion, it looked great but it was reviewed horribly! But Naomi was pleased and I was pleased with it, and so eventually, I was made an associate director of Center Stage.

When Irene was about to leave, a couple of the board members reached out and said: 'Would you like to throw your hat in the ring?' Initially, I was unsure, but then I realized that I had been complaining a lot in Britain. I was moaning about what was being programmed, I was moaning about what was being written, I was moaning about the gatekeepers – the people who ran the institutions. So then I thought, why not?

Now, of course, at the time, I was a playwright with maybe three directing credits to my name. So it was a big risk for them. I'd never been an AD. But I believe playwriting has some profoundly transferable skills, so I ran the building very much like I attack writing a play. You have the first idea and you throw it out there and then you beat it about and then you get to the second draft and then you beat it about some more and you get to the third draft and so on. And you begin to understand whether you have something or you don't. So I would go about artistic programming in that way; I would go about hiring in that way.

How different did it feel making theatre in the United States to making theatre in the UK?
When I started, I thought: 'As long as I listen hard, I might be able to negotiate the differences.' But actually, that turned out not to be true when I got to programming my first season. I started out thinking: 'Well, they've hired me for my British sensibility and I'm a political playwright, so I'm going to create a discursive theatre company for the community.' Our tagline was: 'Welcome to the conversation'. The first thing I did was go to fifty playwrights and say: 'I'm new in this country. Tell me about the United States I've moved to. Write me a monologue and I'll film it and then we'll put it on our website and we'll call it *My America*.' And that generated a nice national buzz in the press. Then I wrote a companion piece to Bruce Norris's *Clybourne Park*, and the *New York Times and The Washington Post* – all the big papers – came down to see it, and the theatre was getting attention it had never had before. Then PBS came and made a documentary about us and that was huge – a million people saw our work across the United States. So we were getting all of these national accolades but our subscription dropped in Baltimore. People were going: 'Yeah, that's just not the kind of theatre I want.' And I was a bit like: 'Oh, shit!'

So you had a public profile that was rocketing, but actually the box office was doing exactly the opposite?
Yes. Now some of that was due to the fact that older members of the community had grown weary of my predecessor's programming. She always ensured that one-third of the season was African American. And while Baltimore is 65 per cent African American, Baltimore County is not.

And presumably, a lot of your subscribers came from outside the city?

Totally. And they had started to vote with their feet. So when I got there, we had our lowest ever membership. When I began the job, I thought: 'Here's how I'll programme: I will do one for me – a discursive political thing; and one for them – a populist thing. In that way, everybody gets something.' But when that wasn't working, I went into the next season and I just did everything for them. I pulled out any of the heavy plays and I just put on comedies. And by the time I got to the end of that season, the local press were going: 'Oh, Kwame gets us. Kwame understands.' And that was a really good lesson for me. And now I make sure I programme every one for me *and* every one for them. And I just take different things from it. If they leave laughing, then that's for me. I made them laugh. If they leave discussing the play, then I made them discuss the play. And once I got to that understanding, I knew that by season three, I had to gently move the audience to where I wanted them to be, but also I had to respect where they are. That was a really big lesson to learn.

At the Gate, I remember one show in particular that I programmed purely because I thought it would do well audience- and press-wise, which it did. But I knew that I didn't really believe in it and neither did my team. So despite it being a big hit, it felt like a really hollow experience. How did that second season feel to you?

It was a hollow experience. It was hard to look at myself in the mirror. But I believed in the long game. And so when I got to the end of the season and I saw that we had got back on track, I felt good about it. It was worth it. I remember a journalist from the *Baltimore Sun* had written something saying: 'I fear for our state theatre.' That was only by play number 3 or something! So I called them to lunch and said: 'Give me a chance, bro. Give me a moment. You know, I'm only just discovering this.' I think the biggest thing I learned about was the importance of listening. I would send staff out to listen to the audience after every show. I would send staff to walk to the car park and overhear what people were saying. They'd have to go into the toilets and listen to what was going on. Our security would tell me what people were saying on their way in and way out. I learned to listen very hard.

One word that we use a lot in the theatre – and you have already touched on it a little – is 'community'. Baltimore has an incredibly divided community: along lines of race and wealth and so on. Can you talk a little more about the role that you think Center Stage has in relation to that?

The ambition is to say to those who don't come to the theatre very often: 'You're welcome. Here's something for you.' It's important also that those who are from the wealthiest demographic come into the theatre and go: 'This is for everyone and I'm sitting next to someone whom I might not have expected to be there, but how interesting to see this play through their lens.' For me, it was really important that Center Stage was seen as really caring about the community. So, for example, when we did the musical *Marley*, the uprising in response to the death of Freddie Gray[1] happened while we were in tech. And so I asked the cast: 'Listen, can we go out to the very place, Penn North, where the pain is most manifested? Let's go down. Let's play the show.' And so we did. These people would not be coming to Center Stage, so we sang all the songs from the show – singing Bob Marley while the National Guard walked by. A local councillor said: 'You can't do this. You're going to cause an uprising.' We said: 'We will do it.' We could see people across the road at the subway station dancing, cars were beeping and a video of it all went viral. And what that meant was that the people of Baltimore knew that I was serious. We were not just saying: 'Hey, let's do a community show.' They knew that I was serious and that these songs would contribute to healing. Going out there and trying to heal was our job – as one of the pillars of the community. From that moment, people understood what we're doing.

For the last two years now, we've had a mobile unit that goes out and serves the prisons, the homeless shelters, the women's shelters and so on. We tour for three or four weeks and then come back and perform the show in the theatre. We're taking art to people because everybody deserves access to art. And it's really interesting because my first instinct when I started thinking about going to prisons was: 'Oh, I've read this brilliant play by a guy called Lemon Andersen about men in jail and how they're negotiating their masculinity.' And so I thought: 'I

[1]An African American man whose death, while in police custody, led to widespread protests in Baltimore and beyond.

want to take that to them.' And then, I realized, actually, that's not what they want. What they want when art comes to them is to be taken out of that world. And seeing people in prison just dig on the storytelling, dig on the joy, it was tremendous.

So I take the art to the community and I ask wealthier members of the community to sponsor that. And then, I ask other members of the community to come to the theatre. For instance, over the last three or four years, we have had people coming to the theatre from zip codes in the city that never came before. I remember once walking in and seeing a black, 55-year-old female in a fur coat there. And I had a play on called *Twisted Melodies*. And I thought: 'This is a hit.' Because I knew that if people with disposable income who would dress up to go to the theatre were coming, then the word of mouth was good. And it was a record-breaking show. We're probably going to do a big community show in the park with professional actors and community actors as my last show. And that will be my parting gift to Center Stage. So making sure that people know that the community is everything is really important to me.

It's one thing to be bringing different groups of people in to see a show. But do you think that has an impact in terms of encouraging and building trust or bonds between those different groups of people?

I think ultimately that's what we want, right? At the moment, I've got a talking table in my lobby. Basically, it's a round table that has eight to ten chairs around it. At the end of the show, if you want to talk about it with someone you don't know, you just go and sit there. And then, someone else whom you didn't go to the theatre with can come and you can start having a conversation with them. That for me is that philosophy made manifest: it's not enough for me just to bring in separate communities; I need them to talk to each other.

How do you approach programming an overall season's worth of work? Do you start with the repertoire or do you start with the artists?

I generally start with trying to seek the zeitgeist. Trying to think: 'What will people be talking about next year?' This forces you to move away from the immediate and into thinking about metaphor. And so I would often have themes: the current season for instance is the Season of

Community. That second season I spoke about was called the Season of Joy. So I would absolutely start with trying to ride the zeitgeist – finding the plays that I thought might speak to that. Also I would find the plays that might be on in New York that everybody was going: 'This is a magnificent play.' And then as I went through the process of having to ratify it all via the finance committee and the executive committee and then the board, I invariably would attach directors to plays at that stage. So I would start with the play.

Whereas for the Young Vic, it is still very early days. But I think I'm going to try and mix that model up and wait for directors and writers and actors to come to me and say I really want to do this or that play. Obviously there will be anchors for that first season – I'm thinking about the anchor of my first play and possibly my last play – but in between them I'm waiting to see who comes with something that tickles me and tickles them.

You mentioned the need to ratify your programme with the board. Could you say a little more about how you work with them in general?

I like to make sure that I'm using their expertise. Many of them have travelled and seen more plays than I have from across the country and the wider world. I want them to be able to come to me and recommend things they like. An example is *One Night In Miami*. That came from a board member being in LA and seeing it in a 99-seat theatre and then telling me to fly out there and see it. So I always make sure that the board are part of the process. And the kind of play you do affects the bottom line, and that bottom line is ultimately their direct responsibility.

More generally, I'll always write our plans up on the board in our artistic space and encourage everyone to come in and give me their take. As I say in any building that I run, I'd rather hear it in the rehearsal room than read about it in the *New York Times*.

Yes, I've always believed that, when programming, you need to foster a sense of shared ownership over everything. I would encourage all my staff to read the plays we were thinking of doing. And in one case actually, in my final season, I made a decision not to programme a play I was very keen on, on the

basis that my marketing officer, a very brilliant young woman, had read it and had some really specific political objections to it and she made a really persuasive case about why we shouldn't do it.
I do that all the time. I ask all my senior staff to read the play with two heads. Number one is to think how they can do their job with this specific play, and number two is to think: if they were just an audience member, how would they respond to it? And so what invariably happens is that I get responses that I would never had otherwise heard. In fact I programmed a show last season, despite my artistic intern saying: 'You should not do this play; it's offensive.' But I didn't really hear her. Yet she was right, and my audience went crazy. They said to me: 'How dare you put this rape on stage? How can you support this misogyny? How dare you?' It was a huge thing, and it was one of the first times that I hadn't listened.

Did you tell your intern that you should have listened?
Totally and utterly. She had left by then, but I called her and I asked her to come and see the show. And she said: 'This is how I feel about it, and I told you this is how others would feel about it.' And I apologized.

It can be hard to hear that stuff, can't it be? It's easy to not hear the things you don't want to hear, but you have to stop yourself from doing that. You have to force yourself to listen to somebody who tells you that you're wrong.
Yes. But you also have to really believe it. Just because someone says you're wrong you can't just go: 'Okay, I'm wrong and therefore I will swing with the wind.' But in this specific case, with my male blinkers, I simply did not see what she was saying. So when it comes to patriarchy I know I have to listen harder than I would do if those issues were not in the play.

It is clear from much of what you have written and said publicly that diversity is a key issue for you. What does that word mean to you? Where do you feel you've been most successful and what do you think are the biggest challenges for you as an artist and for the buildings that you run?
In terms of success, when I arrived at Center Stage I was one of only two senior managers of colour. There was me and this one other person

who worked in marketing – and that, to me, was unacceptable. But what I didn't do was go around saying: 'I need to diversify, I need to diversify.' I just did it. We made sure that the dog whistle attached to some of the work said to people who were interested in black excellence: 'This is a place for you to come and work. This is a place where you may not have to feel as alienated as you do.'

What was that dog whistle?

We did a video project called *My America Two* in 2015 during the slew of young black men being killed. We created a rapid response unit and we filmed a monologue or duologue on the spot where Trayvon Martin was killed, on the spot where Michael Brown was killed, on the spot where Eric Garner was killed. Literally on the spot. And the plays all had different perspectives: one was from the point of view of the police, one was from the point of view of the mother of a police officer who was caught, one was shot while the funeral was happening for the nine people killed in Charleston. And we filmed those things and put them out on the web. I think that let people know what we were doing without talking about it.

Now a third, if not 40 per cent, of my senior management are people of colour; my associate artistic director is a black female Muslim. At the level below that, a third again are African American. And now when you go into the building, it looks diverse. So I don't talk about diversity. I don't shout about it. I just do it. I fundamentally believe that people who have come from diverse backgrounds have a perspective that I need to hear.

What draws you to the Young Vic? What are your ambitions for that theatre?

When I arrived in Baltimore and I knew that we were going to go into a capital campaign, I got ten of my board members to fly over to the UK and visit the Young Vic. And I said to them: 'This is the energy that I want in our theatre.' And in some ways that makes taking over harder because David Lan has done so much and hit so much out the park. So what I'm doing right now is I'm just listening. I don't have a plan. You know I have a couple of things in my brain about a possible destination, but I've got to road-test them with the staff, I've got to road-test them with the board and I've got to road-test them with constituents. I'm madly frightened and madly excited at the same time. My fear is about the quality of my listening. Can I listen well enough and move everything out of the way so that I can hear what the audience wants? With each show, the audience has to be won.

Finally, who are the artistic directors that have inspired you?
The National's former artistic director Nick Hytner and his executive director Nick Starr. When we transferred *Elmina's Kitchen* to the West End, Nick Starr would have me sit in meetings with the producers so that I could understand what producing was. And he made money feel clean for me. He made me go: 'Oh producing is honourable. It's not just about trying to save money; it's about creating the facility to create the art.' Also, Oskar Eustis at The Public is a man after my own heart. His mind is phenomenal. I think I've done four productions there, and each time I feel like I'm going to school. I use all the lessons that he ever taught me. He has made me a better artist.

9
DAVID LAN

David Lan was artistic director of the Young Vic Theatre from 2000 to 2017. Situated near Waterloo in London, the Young Vic produces a range of new plays and radical revivals of classics. It has a 450-seat main house and two studios that seat 150 and 70, respectively.

Can you tell me about your journey, personally and professionally, to becoming artistic director of the Young Vic?
I grew up in South Africa. When I was eleven or twelve, my father gave me a box of conjuring tricks and I discovered I was quite good at doing magic. I read lots of books on card tricks and ordered magic effects from Davenports – a magic shop in London. I think it was obvious that I had some performing skill. Also, my mother was very keen on theatre and I found among the books on her shelf a copy of *Waiting for Godot* and a collection of four plays by Ibsen. Modernism was the first theatre style I knew anything about.

Then I got into puppets. When I was fourteen or fifteen I worked with a professional touring marionette company. We did *The Little Mermaid*. I operated the Little Mermaid herself. So although I didn't realize this at the time, in retrospect I must have been quite a good operator as all the other operators were grown-ups.

Because I grew up under apartheid in South Africa, all theatres were segregated. So the leading playwrights of Europe and the United States wouldn't let their plays be performed there. One exception was the theatre of the University of Cape Town. Due to some glitch in the law, the university was open – anyone could study there, so the theatre on campus was integrated. Not that there were many black people around – they couldn't afford to go to university – but there were some. This theatre became one of the intellectual centres of the city because there you could see plays by Brecht and Arthur Miller and Jean-Paul Sartre and so on. Though performed by students, the casts were often augmented by professional actors.

As a kid, I worked in this theatre's workshop. I used to help make sets – stretching and priming canvas and so on – during school holidays. All the other people working at that level in the workshop were black or what we called 'coloured'. In an endemically racist society, that experience was formative.

Like everybody, when I was at school I acted and directed. I was borrowed by other schools to act in their plays or even – absurdly – to advise on productions. So I wanted to be an actor, and when I left school I went to the drama department at the University of Cape Town and trained as an actor for two years, at the same time as doing a BA degree. Then. In my second year, partly because I'd been drawn into the radical student life of the time, I realized that what I was more interested in were the sociological and political questions to do with the nature of the society I lived in. I had always written plays and I directed a bit at university and so I thought: 'I'm not going to be an actor.'

I came to England without really knowing what I wanted to do. My parents thought I was going to train as a director. What I actually did was go to the LSE to study social anthropology. At the same time my plays were picked up by the Royal Court. The artistic director then was Oscar Lewenstein. Nicholas Wright, who was one of the reasons I came to England and whom I was living with, was running the Theatre Upstairs, which he had started. I submitted plays to the Court under a pseudonym. They turned down the first of these (it was produced by the Almost Free Theatre) but they decided to do the second, so then I said: 'Aha, it's me!'

Over the next few years, plays and adaptations I wrote were produced by the Court, the National, the Almeida, the RSC. Through this whole time I always had the idea that I'd like to run a theatre I had no idea how to get to do it. As well as Oscar and Nick, I'd watched other people run the Court. I had a sense of what running a theatre could be like.

But I was also getting deep into social anthropology. I had a long period – ten years off and on – doing research in post-war Zimbabwe, writing a PhD, writing a book – still puzzling about the questions that had occurred to me while working in the scenic workshop. Why do some people have power and others don't? How did that happen? How is power maintained?

And you were doing TV documentaries for the BBC as well, weren't you?

I did a little bit of film writing and script doctoring for Channel Four. One film that I co-wrote for them, based on the Joseph Conrad novel *Under Western Eyes,* was made by an Israeli director. The original is set between St Petersburg and Zurich. Our version, the story of a Palestinian radical who betrays his cause, was set between Tel Aviv and Berlin. Later I worked with the brilliant documentarist Adam Low on BBC drama documentaries. We researched together in Mozambique, Angola, Namibia, and I wrote and he directed. Then I wrote, directed and produced one myself in Nigeria.

So you'd look at a real story and write a fictional account of it and then it would be performed by the actual people?

Yes, people played themselves or they played people they knew and were close to. The one I made on my own in Nigeria was a bit different. Nigel Williams commissioned it for BBC Omnibus. The actor Lennie James played himself on a quest, starting in an antique shop in Portobello Road where he finds a little bronze Benin mask and tracks it back to where it came from in a workshop in the extraordinary semi-feudal Benin City in central Nigeria.

Then I made a completely different film, also for Omnibus, about the redevelopment of the Royal Court Theatre. This was now the mid-1990s. I was 'writer in residence' there, working with Stephen Daldry, the then artistic director. He gave me the best job description ever: 'Do what you like until you meet resistance.' So I talked to Omnibus and they gave me a little camera and I filmed everything over the course of a year. We edited it into a diary which ended when the theatre closed for its redevelopment. I learned quite a bit about construction, which was useful later on.

And by observation I learned something about running a theatre. When I had plays produced I could watch the artistic directors of those theatres – Daldry, Jonathan Kent/Ian McDiarmid, Trevor Nunn, Richard Eyre – doing the job in their contrasting ways.

One of the advantages of being a playwright is that, if you're lucky, you get to work with many different kinds of director. I'd had plays and translations directed by Nicholas Wright, Max Stafford-Clark, Katie Mitchell, Nicholas Hytner, Andrei Serban, Howard Davies. I worked with Peter Brook on an idea for a film that never got made but which now, all these years later, he is turning into a play.

I went to Sue Higginson who was running the National Theatre Studio and said: 'I want to direct *Pericles* by William Shakespeare.' All my friends said: 'Oh no, that's too difficult.' Which it was. Sue gave me three weeks. I worked with actors in the NT company. A few people came to see it. It's a wonderful play about everything in life that matters. My anthropological knowledge was useful for working out what the mysterious first act is all about and perhaps a little of what is great about the play somehow came through.

Giles Croft, who was running the Watford Palace, either saw my *Pericles* or was told about it and asked me to direct *The Glass Menagerie* by Tennessee Williams. I would never have thought of doing it. In terms of the work I've done since, that experience was interesting to me. I find that a powerful way to create a season is to suggest to directors ideas for plays they wouldn't themselves have thought of. Often it's in the unexpectedness of the meeting of play and director that something revealing occurs.

Caroline Maude, who was then executive director at the Young Vic, saw my Watford show. Tim Supple, the artistic director, had commissioned a translation of something, which, when it came in, they didn't like. So they had an unexpected gap in their programme. I got a phone call from Caroline asking: 'Would you like to do *'Tis a Pity She's a Whore* by John Ford?' Again, I would never have thought of this. While I was rehearsing it, Tim announced he was leaving – though not as a consequence, I think!

My stage manager asked: 'Are you going to apply?' I said: 'Of course not.' It hadn't occurred to me, but then I thought: 'What a good idea.' I asked Caroline for her view and she didn't fall over laughing. Once I'd decided I wanted it, I did a lot of work to get it.

What kind of work?

For one thing Stephen Daldry rehearsed the interview with me a number of times. He asked lots of hard questions. Some of what I learned over those days has been useful to me ever since. For example, he asked one question – I can't remember what it was – and I gave a negative answer of some kind and he said: 'Why are you being negative? Never be negative.' I try never to be.

I was obviously a marginal candidate. Years later the chair of the board told me I'd been his 'wild card'. Stephen called to say that one of the other two shortlisted people was strongly tipped to get the job. So when I went in for the second interview I had nothing to lose. Both the other two candidates subsequently got jobs running major theatres. When my appointment was announced it was a serious non-event. There was a half-inch article in *The Stage*: 'An insignificant but curious thing has happened.' I paraphrase.

One of the first things I realized was that the company didn't have anything like enough income. We received something like £400,000 from the Arts Council, which was a substantial amount of money but nothing like enough to run a full programme. I remember a very early conversation with Caroline when it dawned on me that the cost of salaries and overheads was about the same as the grant and the box office income. So how do we afford to do shows? They did almost no fundraising in those days.

So you just had public funding and box office?
The way they had made it work was to do maybe two of their own productions a year. The rest of the year they presented existing shows from companies such as the Oxford Stage Company and the RSC. The problem was that all the touring work was conceived for proscenium or thrust stage houses. Although it often needed to be adapted somewhat to play the Young Vic, most of the time the Young Vic auditorium was used in the most conventional ways.

And at this point the Young Vic had only one space, presumably?
It had the main auditorium seating around 400 and it had a rehearsal room, often used as a studio, seating about sixty that was given over to small-scale tours. By the time I started, the building, which had been built thirty years before with a five-year life expectancy, was seriously falling down. One evening, during a show, rain got through the roof onto the lighting board. The local council was always threatening to close us.

So the job I was given was to run the company and to get the building rebuilt. But nobody was going to give us the resources to do it unless there was a clear reason. I had to figure out what this place could do that no other place had thought of. Of course it had to be something worth doing.

Because I was new to directing, I thought: 'Well, if I'm going to learn how to direct, why doesn't everyone?' Few other theatres were seriously engaged with directing; everyone focused on writers. The question of the day was: 'In theatre, who is the primary artist?' – a pointless question. It doesn't matter where the big ideas come from so long as there are big ideas.

For me, what is emotionally and intellectually powerful is when there is a disjunction between the play as *play* – as 'text' – and the moment in which that play finds its audience, its first audience in the case of a new play or its new audiences over the decades. What matters is locating the relationship between the original moment of creation and the present moment of theatre making. I'm interested in the relationship between the director's consciousness and the consciousness of the play. That's where energy is.

I quickly came to understand that the job of producing is not to try and replicate the moment in which the play was written – period costume, period manners, etc. – but to try to imagine the *effect* the creation of a new piece of theatre had on its first audience – and to get that to happen *now*.

Are there specific productions that you had seen when you were young that you felt achieved this?

When I was fifteen my kind and generous parents brought my sister and me to Europe on holiday. We spent a few weeks in London. With my family I saw a Harry Secombe musical called, I think, *The Four Musketeers* at Drury Lane – and then I would sneak off and see the shows I wanted to see. As part of Peter Daubeny's 1967 World Theatre Season at the Aldwych Theatre, I saw Lorca's *Yerma* directed by the Argentinian Victor Garcia with the leading Spanish actress of the day Nuria Espert performing entirely on a large ochre-coloured trampoline. I can only remember it through the eyes of a fifteen-year-old but I still say it was one of the greatest productions I've ever seen. I remember it moment by moment; it's burned into my heart.

I came to live here in 1972. In 1974 Peter Hall's National Theatre brought two productions from the Théâtre National Populaire (TNP) from Villeurbanne. One was *Tartuffe* directed by Roger Planchon who ran the TNP. The other was *La Dispute* by Marivaux directed by Patrice Chereau. I remember great bursts of both. The TNP under Planchon – its aesthetic, its ethos, its political purpose as I understand it – has been a big influence on me as an artistic director.

When I was very young, I saw *Tartuffe*, one of Tyrone Guthrie's last productions, at the National with John Gielgud and Robert Stephens. It had an abstract design by René Allio. Everyone hated it. I *loved* it. I can remember it scene by scene. Guthrie is the great forgotten hero. It was his conception of theatre architecture that created the whole tradition of thrust theatres in this country: Chichester, Sheffield, the Bolton Octagon, here.

All these memories fed into my thinking about the 'directors programme' we started. But as well as coming up with the big idea, in terms of getting the building restored, a problem I faced was that the unique value of the Young Vic's auditorium, which is a work of architectural genius, had been forgotten.

It's funny because you've been talking about the theatre being used as a proscenium arch and then as a deep thrust, but I don't think about it like that at all. For me it is one of the most flexible spaces in London.

Well, the original building was put up cheaply and quickly. The thrust is set in huge blocks of concrete. When we rebuilt, we explored the possibility of getting rid of a lot of the concrete but we didn't do that. I don't like 'black boxes'. I hate great big empty would-be 'neutral' spaces painted black. They're depressing. One of the things our architect, Steve Tompkins, and I liked about the auditorium here is that the original concrete structures create a certain amount of resistance. They provoke artists working in the room to find interesting and original solutions.

I felt the same at the Gate. The space used to drive me up the wall because it was narrower at one end than the other. But I would always say that the Gate is the wrong shape to be a theatre, which means it's exactly the right shape to be a theatre.

I couldn't agree more. Of course, a well-designed proscenium theatre is also a great thing. The Odeon in Paris is the most beautiful theatre in the world. But in order to make the case for the future of the Young Vic, it became my policy to say to directors and designers: 'Treat this space as though there's never been a show produced here before. Truly start from scratch. Understand the architecture. Where will you put the stage?' I've produced more than a hundred shows in the space but we still find ways to use it that we've never thought of before. It's a magnificent auditorium; we know that now, but in my early days I had to make the case for it by producing all kinds of crazy shows that couldn't or wouldn't happen anywhere else.

The other important thing I had to do was take control of the repertoire. I didn't want touring shows or anyone else's shows. I had to say: 'No, we don't have much money but somehow I will make all the important decisions. If I'm wrong they can sack me.' The trick was to find ways of co-producing. We co-produced with everybody, first in London, then in the UK and then all over the world starting with Iceland. The game is to produce with other people's money – but there has to be genuine mutual benefit or it won't work in the long run or even in the short run.

I was forty-eight when I got the job, which is old to run your first theatre. But the good side of that was I'd been around and I knew a lot of people, so if I didn't know how to do something, which was most of the time, I knew whom to ask. And one of the wonderful, life-affirming things about working in the arts is the generosity you find there.

I've always been struck by how political and progressive the work at the Young Vic is. Currently, hanging on the balcony outside this theatre, there's a rainbow LGBTQI flag, a Black Lives Matter flag, a European flag and a Refugees flag. Has that element of the work always felt essential to you?

I grew up in the South African theatre of the 1960s and 1970s. So one of the values of theatre that seems natural to me is that it gives voice to those who would otherwise be silenced. And in this country, I grew up at the Royal Court. The Court in those days was distinguished by its bolshiness, by its conviction that no one else was any good *at all*. It was a left-wing theatre; it was instinctively oppositional.

The whole point of a publicly funded theatre is that it challenges the market place. Public investment allows you to create a relationship with artists and audience based on risk. You just have to understand the risk you're taking. You have to make sure you know, as best you can, where the risk is. You have to control whatever you can control – and you have to *be there all the time* so you have the best chance of knowing the right moment to make the perfect intervention to get the ideal result from all the elements you can't – and anyway don't want to – control.

In the early years of doing this job I bumped into Kim Evans who was senior at the Arts Council at the time. I asked her how she felt I was doing, and she said: 'If you're not bold, our work is meaningless.' I was grateful for that. Somehow the work I produced had to express what I believed to be true about the world. I only produced what I love. If I didn't love it, I wouldn't know how to produce it so we didn't do it. That kept me going.

How does it feel to know that you will be leaving the Young Vic soon?

Over the course of my time here, I've had a number of ideas and tried to explore them as fully as I could. A lot of the things we've done here are now happening in other places. And that's great. But you have to stay ahead of the game. A theatre has always to be 'hot'; it always has to surprise. So if I stayed we'd need a big new idea. And the question was: 'Am I going to find that new idea or is it someone else's turn?' Eighteen years is a long time. I would hate to stay so long people are going: 'Poor sod, doesn't he realise … ?'

Finally, who are the artistic directors who have inspired you?

Nick Wright constantly producing the hip and the provocative was formative – as was the fact that he worked *so hard.* Stephen Daldry's boldness was a key teaching – as was that of Jonathan Kent and Ian McDiarmid at the Almeida.

I've always found Peter Hall fascinating, driven, as he seems to have been, by – well, 'class hatred' probably doesn't describe it – a combination of class hatred and class adoration. Richard Eyre's championing of brilliant younger directors was epoch-making: Daldry, Katie Mitchell, Declan Donnelan, Simon McBurney, Deborah Warner. I barely knew her but I admired what Clare Venables achieved at Sheffield. Our Clare studio is named after her.

But that's just the UK. I based my choice of shows on the left-humanist repertoire of the TNP under Planchon. Luc Bondy became a close friend; I learned a vast amount from his wise wilfulness. Brook because, in his own words, he 'just follows his nose'. The greatest of all, of course, was Diaghilev. He understood that all you need to do to create great work is gather great people. Just persuade the best possible artists to get together in a room, and then you can go on holiday.

10
TOM MORRIS

Tom Morris was artistic director of Battersea Arts Centre (BAC) from 1995 to 2004. BAC has multiple performance spaces and is dedicated to supporting formally inventive artists and devised theatre. He has been artistic director of the Bristol Old Vic since 2009. The theatre has a 540-seat auditorium and a smaller studio space.

What was your journey to becoming artistic director of the Bristol Old Vic?

At university I ran a theatre company with a couple of friends. We put shows on in Edinburgh and on the London Fringe. I then spent some time researching for a PhD, and while I was doing that I started to write journalism as a way to find out about theatre. Eventually, despite really loving teaching, I drifted out of academia and started writing about and producing theatre. I brought over a theatre company from Tel Aviv to London, and I worked for the Lyric Theatre in Hammersmith when they were trying to bring over the Maly Theatre from St Petersburg.

A key moment in terms of my shift from writing about theatre to producing it came when I went to see a company from Poland called Gardzienice performing in St Paul's Church in Hammersmith. I found myself writing a review that said: 'Whatever you're doing, stop! Book a ticket. It's only on for three more nights, just go!' And I came to understand that in my writing about theatre, what I was basically doing was producing, but just not doing it very effectively: I was trying to manage a relationship between the work and an audience. And that, at its most fundamental level, is what producers do.

So I decided I wanted to run a theatre. Around that time, the job of director of BAC came up. I was reviewing for *Time Out* in London and had seen shows there, and I knew that it had huge potential. But it was very hard to get an audience to go there. I actually missed the application deadline at first. But I got in touch and asked if I could apply late, and they called me in for an interview. What I didn't know was that anyone on the shortlist with any experience had asked to see the theatre's financial information and had then withdrawn their applications! That's how it was they were able to interview me and, I guess, partly why they ended up offering me the job.

So when I arrived, there was no money. Nonetheless, there was this extraordinary opportunity to position the theatre in a distinct space and to make the kind of work that I was passionate about. It seemed obvious to me that if all you had was space rather than money, you needed to find the artists who didn't have space and find a way to balance the risk with the opportunity – by working with them on a box office split. It wasn't rocket science, and I certainly wasn't the first person to do it. But it defined the project as being about identifying extraordinary artists and giving them space to make the work they were most passionate about. We also defined ourselves in opposition to what was, at that point, a quite well-funded new writing scene in London – with the Royal Court, the Bush, the Soho Theatre and so on. We realized that there was a gap in the market for people who might be devising or making theatre in ways that didn't start with a finished script.

Gradually, we evolved a methodology of programming and artist development from this simple starting point. A key moment in this was when I went to see a sharing of some research towards an adaptation of *The Mouse and His Child* that Improbable Theatre were doing as part of the Barclay's New Stages programme at the Royal Court. Afterwards, I got talking to Improbable's two artistic directors, Phelim McDermott and Julian Crouch, about their process. I learnt from them that some of the artists who most inspired me (as they did) created work through a process of iterative uncertainty. And that if they could show it to an audience before it was finished, that might help them to find out what it might become. So as part of the British Festival of Visual Theatre (based in those days at BAC), we introduced a strand of unfinished work, which we called 'Sights Unseen'. And that then developed into a something which we called the 'scratch program', which I guess became the defining methodology of the theatre.

At the same time as all of that, the theatre's underlying financial situation was gradually emerging. I'd thought it was disastrous. In fact, it was nearly terminal. We only survived because of two extraordinary shifts in the funding climate. First came Lottery funding, introduced by John Major. This enabled us to put some money into the building, to buy some proper technical equipment and to pay off some of our deficit. Secondly, there was the Arts Council's Theatre Review, which led to massive funding reforms in the late 1990s. This review identified the need for investment in art form development and gave us the platform to argue that BAC was the place for this to happen. Without those two funding revolutions, we would have gone bust.

Even after the organization was stabilized, resources were still fairly limited. But I've always felt that the ground rules of subsidy are: 'If you've got no funding, share the space you've got. If you've got lots of funding, commission the work. If you've got a little bit of funding, buy beer and invite the artist to come talk.' And so that's what we did. We created the Artists Brainstorming Group, which was composed of writers, directors, composers, performers and others who made us excited about what they might do next. We had meetings where we'd ask: 'What should we be making work about?' Ideas would come up, and then we'd say: 'Okay, anyone who wants to talk about this idea, go to that table over there and talk to Phelim McDermott or Suzy Willson or Erica Whyman or Benji Reid or whoever had had the idea.' And if it was a good idea, and could harness the goodwill and energy of the artists who were in the room, we would do it. This helped me realize that if you engage the passion of artists who have few resources with the right provocation, then something extraordinary and unpredictable can happen, which is exactly how the BAC opera strand evolved, from which *Jerry Springer: The Opera* emerged.

Eventually I started to wonder whether these experiments might work on a bigger scale, and so I applied to run the Bristol Old Vic in 2002. But they showed me their plans for the redevelopment of the theatre and I really felt they weren't right and told them so, and they didn't ask me back for a second interview.

What was wrong with them?

Bristol Old Vic is an exquisite eighteenth-century theatre. It's the oldest working theatre in the English-speaking world. Yet remarkably, in 1970, half of it – all the backstage area – had been knocked down to build a huge flytower. In the 1970s they were able to make these massive sets and fly them in and out, but as a result all the action had to take place far upstage – a long way away from the audience. All of the intimacy of the original theatre was lost, the sightlines didn't work, the pit was too low, etc. And people were mystified as to why it was so hard to make a show work in there. Yet the plans the board showed me did nothing to fix that at all. Instead they wanted to build a new 600-seat theatre on the roof. So they'd have two similarly sized theatres and not enough funding! It was absolutely nuts.

But around that time, Nick Hytner took over at the National. To his extraordinary credit, he'd done some kind of internal audit of his skills and knowledge and essentially come to the conclusion that (where X is the range of work the National needed, and Y was his prodigious expertise): 'X minus Y might leave a gap that included some of the work that was going on at BAC.' So after a series of conversations, he invited me to join as an associate. I hadn't worked anywhere remotely like the National Theatre up to that point, but I went there three days a week and had this extraordinary privilege to be a kind of licensed maverick in their planning meetings. My job was to ask questions which no experienced person would ask and find work for the programme that was made through non-traditional processes. It was amazing. I took Nick to see work by Punchdrunk and Shunt, Melly Still, Kneehigh and Handspring and worked out which artists and which ideas he wanted me to take forward. The perfect job in theatre.

Eventually you did become AD of Bristol Old Vic. How did that come about?

By that point, I'd made several shows that had played here in Bristol. So I knew more about what I thought was wrong with the setup but also about the absolutely unique atmosphere of that auditorium. Historically and architecturally it sits at an intermediate stage between a Shakespearean Globe-type theatre and a proscenium arch theatre – both intimate and yet somehow revelling in the company of its audience. I knew by then that there were things you could do in that theatre which you couldn't do anywhere else.

I also knew that the theatre was difficult to run. It had closed in 2007 for a number of reasons: It had been chronically underfunded; it had a really crazy governance structure with two separate boards – one looking after the building and one looking after the art; there were a series of shows that didn't work; and there had been an overdue capital project which hadn't quite landed. In my view, when theatres go wrong it is always the board's fault – because that's where the buck stops. In the end, all these things are symptoms of failed governance. If the person who's leading the organization isn't leading it properly, and if things are going awry, it's the board's job to sort it out.

So the Arts Council suspended its grant. And there was a whole campaign in response to this and a man called Dick Penny in Bristol agreed to become the new chair of Bristol Old Vic and gradually started to sort it out. He got the Arts Council to suspend their judgement (which really might have been to stop funding the theatre altogether) while he commissioned a report and business plan for its future.

This was all happening while I was still at the National but I'd written to the Bristol Old Vic when it got into trouble and offered to help in any way I could. Dick found my letter and asked me to come and help write the business plan and to brainstorm about what the theatre might be. And through that I learnt that around this beautiful theatre there was also a really complicated, fractured city. And there was a broken or incomplete connection between the theatre and the city. But crucially, there was also a concentration of creative people here – with artists looking to do cross art form things, and a highly curious audience who might be attracted to a forward-looking theatre. So the starting point here was an organization that was clearly broken, but nonetheless, there were some very exciting ingredients that might mend it. Then, when Dick decided to advertise the artistic director job, I applied for it, and crucially Emma Stenning, who had been executive director at BAC, applied for the role of executive director at the same time. Dick and the board believed in us as a double act and that's how I ended up here.

How do you go about putting together a season of work for this theatre? Are you led by the artist or the audience?

I'm still learning about that. I've never quite escaped the ethos that motivated and inspired me at BAC: finding the most extraordinary artists I can, talking to them about what they want to do and then weaving a programme out of that. Part of my reason for coming here was that I'd done that on a small scale at BAC and then I'd worked at the National Theatre which had huge resources by comparison and which had enabled me to produce and direct big shows. So I wanted to see whether I could combine those two things.

It's interesting. Nick Hytner came to Bristol a few months ago and I did a Q&A with him about his book *Balancing Acts*. Somebody asked a question about whether his approach was artist first or programme first. And he said: 'It's always programme first. You work out the rep, and then you work out who's going to do it.' And I thought: 'Well, that's not quite my approach.' What I've been trying to learn while I've been here is how to marry and balance those two approaches. That's been the journey through the whole process of rebuilding the theatre and re-engaging the audience.

In terms of how that builds into a programme, it was clear from the beginning that we had to make the main house programme as exciting and successful as we could. If we don't do that, if we don't make shows that everyone is talking about, then we can't do anything. We can't fundraise, we can't reestablish our reputation and in the end we won't survive. The things that have done that best – *A Midsummer Night's Dream, Jane Eyre, Peter Pan, The Grinning Man, A Long Day's Journey into Night* – have all been 'artist-led' projects. But if those projects don't sit within a balanced programme, the organization really struggles to stay afloat.

Alongside that, I've always absolutely insisted on an outreach programme that is front-footedly engaging people from every borough in the city. In January 2017, there was some research published that said Bristol was the most segregated city in the UK – though, paradoxically, that came out at the same time as the *Sunday Times* reporting that Bristol had been voted the 'happiest place to live'. This outreach programme, currently under threat from Local Authority cuts, is absolutely vital to the mission and ambition of the theatre. We have to be the meaningful champions of creative opportunity for everyone in the city. And if we can't make good that promise, we don't deserve to be here.

The third element of the programme is Bristol Ferment. This is strongly based on the scratch process and is designed to give voice-finding opportunities to the extraordinary artists who are knocking around in Bristol. Similarly, the health of our core programme depends on the refreshment, challenge and inspiration it gets from the artists making work in the Bristol Ferment. So the overall shape of the programme in Bristol depends on the successful interweaving of these three strands of work.

One word that we use a lot in theatre is 'community'. You've mentioned the segregation in Bristol and you can really see that here. There is a great deal of private wealth but also a severe homelessness problem. How do you serve those different groups and what role do you have as a theatre in terms of cohering those groups together?
It's axiomatic, for me, to understand that theatre exists in the mind of the audience. Strangely, this connects with the horseshoe-shaped space here at Bristol Old Vic. When it was built, it had a big central candelabra, which meant the rest of the audience could see you and you could see them. So the multiple different points of view that different members of the audience had were manifest in the architecture. What that means is that everyone intrinsically knows that their experience of what they're seeing is both coherent with what everyone else is experiencing and also distinctive and theirs. I think the architecture is imaginatively empowering of the audience, and our job on the stage is to promote that as skilfully as we can. It's then up to them to take that experience home and to think about and reflect on it.

Alongside that, we have an obligation as a subsidized theatre to initiate and support a dynamic relationship with people from every bit of the city. And that raises some very interesting questions about what community is – to which I don't yet have all the answers. For instance, last night, I was at a donors' dinner. Lots of the people there are what you'd describe as Bristol 'old money'. And they've always come to the theatre. They say to me: 'We used to come see everything. My mum and my dad brought me. We'd all go out to dinner and then go to the theatre.' And one of the challenges historically for this theatre is that at various points in its history, it has belonged too much to that particular community.

On the other hand, we are currently in the middle of a very concentrated outreach programme in Lockleaze, which is not an affluent part of Bristol. A whole lot of people who've never been to the theatre now come to see plays here and we are doing our job better when they do. But there are real and unresolved questions about how financially sustainable those kinds of initiatives are. The Citizens Theatre in Glasgow famously used to do 50p tickets and so the place was always full with an engaged local audience. The structure of subsidy at that point was able to sustain that, which it isn't now. So we don't know yet how we might fundraise to continue subsidizing the tickets in the face of ongoing and relentless reductions in funding.

But it's absolutely imperative for me that we never give up on that ambition. This theatre has a responsibility to engage with the whole city. Our job is to inspire and empower the imaginations of our audiences across all those constituencies. That's the thing that I hope will define our community: people from lots of different walks of life in Bristol having a shared sense that when they come to the theatre, their response matters and their engagement with what they see onstage and with the other audience members is alive.

We find our selves, currently, at a very particular moment, politically, with Trump in the United States and Brexit in the UK. What role do you think theatre has to play in relation to that?

I'm not really persuaded by instrumental art. But there is an interesting opportunity for political engagement in Bristol around the city's relationship with the transatlantic slave trade – and we've commissioned a play from Giles Tererea about that. And that can make people uncomfortable. If you talk to a liberal middle-class person in Bristol, often they will say: 'Well, it was all awful, clearly. It was a terrible moment in history, but what you need to remember is it was a very different time. People thought differently. We mustn't judge them by our standards because they just simply didn't see it as wrong. It was normal.'

Yet if you read the primary sources, from Thomas Clarkson who arrived here in 1787 to research the abolitionist case, through to Edmund Burke's speeches on the slave trade, it's absolutely clear that everyone knew it was wrong. As Clarkson says: 'It seems everyone thinks the trade is execrable, but no one believes abolition is possible.' So you go: 'Fucking hell, they knew! Of course they knew. Why would they not know that enslaving people and selling them was wrong? Everything in their Bibles would tell them it was wrong. Every precept of the governing morality would tell them it was wrong. They knew it was wrong, but they chose to do it anyway, so we absolutely mustn't let them off the hook.' And if we do that, then we can learn from them. We can ask: 'What are the things that we know are wrong now which we suppress our instincts about?' That might be climate change or immigration or, for some people, animal rights. But the important thing is that finding a way into the topic along those lines can make it accessible for those who are uncomfortable. And, obviously, it's clearly accessible to the black community in Bristol. So by finding the right story for Bristol, we can make connections with everything that is happening, politically, now: from Trump to immigration to Brexit to climate change.

Who are the artistic directors who have influenced or inspired you?

Nick Hytner has been massive for me. He's brilliantly clever and brilliant at assembling and balancing a programme. He also has an astonishing ability to never feel any envy about the other directors whose work he puts on. Counterbalancing him, there is Michael Boyd who was at the RSC at the same time that Nick was at the National. He is much more overtly passionate than Nick. Ideally I'd like to be some sort of combination of the two.

I'm also hugely inspired by the ideology of Kneehigh – the theatre without walls, as it was and as it still is. Bill Mitchell, Emma Rice and Mike Shepherd between them really understood the importance of play in the face of fear and the freedom that might come with that. They understood the responsibilities that a leader needs to take away from an artist at the point where the artist needs to play. So I've learnt a huge amount from them.

And lastly, there is Complicite, which I am on the board of and which is another theatre without walls. Simon McBurney absolutely insists on thoroughness and lack of compromise when it comes to the process of observing the world and of waiting until you know how to articulate what you observe. His rigour can create problems for him and those around him, but in the end it's sublimely inspiring. It's really important that there are, somewhere in our creative firmament, people and organizations that don't compromise and that remind us about what's possible if you do that.

11
JIM NICOLA

Jim Nicola has been artistic director of New York Theatre Workshop since 1988. A 198-seat venue in the East Village in Manhattan, it stages around four productions a year across a variety of new plays, musicals and classical revivals.

Tell me about your journey to becoming artistic director of the Workshop?

Family legend has it that when I was three or four, I expressed a desire to become a minister. This was in the early 1950s – my brothers and I were raised in a Baptist church. But it wasn't the sort of Southern Baptist conservative thing; this was a New England Transcendentalist tradition related to Thoreau and Emerson, which in some ways was quite close to the Quakers. The Baptist practice was really ethical – I remember a lot of social justice activities against the Vietnam War, supporting the Civil Rights Movement and so on. So I think somewhere in that early aspiration of mine, at a subconscious level, was the idea of tending to a flock, of providing sustenance and nurture for a group of people.

But I was a little gay boy who didn't fit in and whose parents in the 1950s were very concerned that I conform to gender expectations, so they made me do all kinds of sports that I was no good at. Then when I was about ten years old, I saw an ad in the local paper for a children's group being formed at the little local theatre and I thought: 'That's it!' I started with the idea of being a performer: an actor or a singer. But somewhere in college I had the great, wonderful experience of understanding in a very vivid way that I was not an actor – that that was to be for other people. So then I started directing.

I went to Tufts University, outside of Boston, and they had a London programme, so I spent two years there: 1970 and 1971. At that point I had barely been out of this country ever and suddenly I was immersed in a different culture, which still felt very 'post-war' – I would walk down the street and see a rubble strewn lot from the Blitz. In fact I remember the Young Vic opened on that block while we were there – it was literally built out of the rubble.

That first weekend in London we went to the RSC, which was a new experience for me. Coming from the United States, if I saw large-scale theatre, it was usually a Broadway musical. But the first thing we saw was Trevor Nunn's *Winter's Tale* with Judi Dench as Hermione and Perdita. The next day we saw a matinee of *Major Barbara* and in the evening, John Barton's very autumnal *Twelfth Night*. To watch all of those actors making theatre on a large scale that wasn't a musical but was actually serious and had poetry and ideas and substance and to which they had dedicated their lives – well I had never experienced anything like that. Also, as part of this programme I went to the Royal Court and I observed a lot there, and that changed my idea of what theatre was. I understood that it could be a bigger thing than just entertainment. It could really be a place to stimulate or provoke people to take action and change things. That was exciting.

Then, when I got to New York after I graduated, the dominant presence was Joe Papp. I became quite infatuated with him and ended up working for him in casting for the New York Shakespeare Festival. He was also the resident producer at Lincoln Center and was regularly doing stuff on Broadway. He was not actually a great director. He kept trying to do it but he was not good at it. It was clear that his genius was for forging space literally and figuratively. In a dynamic city like New York, he could get people's attention and make them come to his building and see the work of these people they'd never heard of, alongside Shakespeare. I could see in him the idea that leading a theatre company was as valid an artistic discipline as playwriting, or directing, or acting. This had not been recognized before, but it was clear that with Joe I was in the company of someone who was a genius at it. The best thing about him was that you never felt he got stale. He was always making choices because he was curious. His theatre started with Shakespeare, and then it was new American writing, and then it was about directors and then it was about British work. He would just keep finding new ideas. It was a big laboratory for him. That's what made it alive and fresh and exciting as an institution.

Then in 1980 I got a fellowship from the National Endowment for the Arts to go to the Arena Stage in Washington, where that great pioneering woman Zelda Fichandler was still in charge and I made a real connection with her. I think that Zelda and Joe were like my mother and father in spirit. In many ways they were the male and the female of each other. She too would direct but was not very good at it and yet also had a similar kind of genius for making a space, making a place. She had more of a European sensibility – she felt there was this great body of world literature that it was important for people to be in touch with on a daily basis. She wasn't comfortable with contemporary writing because she was always judging a new play against the standards of Chekhov, Shaw and so on. We would do twelve to fifteen plays a year in three different spaces in this amazing complex that she had constructed from nothing.

So you've had these two huge influences in your life: Zelda and Joe. How did you then end up at New York Theatre Workshop?
Well, I was directing at Arena Stage and I was directing at a lot of other smaller theatres in Washington. But then this thing of being a minister came back to me – it was really now, in a secular way, reasserting itself. I think it came out of the process of picking seasons at Arena, which had to be this sort of civic theatre that was wide and broad in its tastes and experiences. We had to ask: 'What kind of theatre do we want to be? What experience do we want to provide to our flock?' But some of the decisions that Zelda was making were frustrating to me.

I remember one of the big conflicts was over *The Normal Heart*, Larry Kramer's play – which I thought was a perfect play for the four-sided stage at Arena. Not only was it this incredibly hot play about a very big contemporary issue – because there's a large gay community in DC – but it was like an Ibsen play. So it had a formal interest for a theatre like Arena beyond the more superficial, topical themes of it. But she just couldn't go there – she was too squeamish about gay issues. That was the other thing with both of those giants, Joe and Zelda, I was a part of helping them to engage with their views on homosexuality which were common to that era. So that just was a big blow to me. I felt like this was a really important thing to do in DC but we were backing away from it. Now it's her theatre and that's her right. But I began feeling like maybe this wasn't a paradise that was going to be long lasting for me.

As that feeling started to grow, I got this phone call to come and apply for this job at New York Theatre Workshop. I had seen the work at this theatre and it excited me. But most importantly it was, as far as I could tell, the first theatre in this country to say: 'We are equally as interested in directors as we are in writers.'

It's very evident in your work here that championing amazing directors is key – Ivo van Hove, Sam Gold, Rachel Chavkin. That is relatively unusual in what's quite a literary theatre culture.
Yes. And that comes from Stephen Graham, who founded the organization in 1979 and is still on the board and a major donor. He had been studying dramaturgy at Yale, but he dropped out and came to New York to become a commercial producer with this small group of friends. They wanted to reject the bureaucracy of the not-for-profit theatres which they didn't feel were as responsive or as daring as they could be.

But the problem they ran into was that the plays and the authors and the artists that they liked were never going to make a profit. They were never going to succeed in the commercial world. So his answer was to create this foundation called the Stephen Graham Foundation that would be unlike the existing structure of the not-for-profits. Their problem with those was that the subscription model meant everything was about filling slots. It wasn't about finding this brilliant idea from an artist from which everything should follow. Artists were being asked to compromise too much to fit into that structure. His idea was: 'We'll start with the artist and the structure will follow that.' He also said: 'It's not just about the playwright; it's about the director.' Right from the start of his thinking, the director was central. And that lasted a few years. The idea was that they would pick an artist and say: 'We like you, we want to support you, what do you need?' That might involve small things like helping them out with rent, or buying them a new typewriter, but it could go all the way up to supporting a full production. But they wouldn't become a theatre – they would just give substantial grants. One of the first writers they supported was Harry Kondoleon whose play *Christmas on Mars* got produced at Playwrights Horizons with a sizeable grant.

Eventually they hired a wonderful woman named Jean Passanante to be the director of the foundation, and by 1983 she had pretty much persuaded them they did want to become a theatre, so they incorporated as New York Theatre Workshop. Stephen became the executive director and she was the artistic director until 1988. I loved the work that she did and I loved the thinking that she did. I always remember feeling like if I were to ever run to a theatre, it might be this one.

I felt that between Jean and Stephen, I had this incredible foundation of thinking and values to work with – you start with the artist and to the absolute degree that you can, you let them dictate the structure of everything. And when you have one funder and all the resources come from one mind and one imagination, that's very easy to do. But when you have to persuade this foundation, or this ticket buyer, or that individual to give you fifty bucks, it becomes impossible to do that. You have to be able to tell them what you're going to do, and a programmatic structure has to emerge. I think the thing that we have tried to keep to in that original spirit is to create 'menus'. When you walk in here as an artist, we can say: 'This is the stuff that we have to offer.'

So what is on those menus?

Well, we created this *Usual Suspects* scheme. That was something that came from my Arena days – where I was so grateful for that experience of having company as a young director. I will never forget walking into the first day of rehearsal of a play with seasoned actors in their forties, fifties, sixties, who all had long-term relationships with each other. That was very different from my New York days. You could begin the first day of rehearsal so far beyond where you were with just a pick-up company. I really learned the lesson that theatre making is almost always better if the relationships are continuing. But I also realized that in many ways that was impossible in New York because it's the opposite of what people come to New York for. Artists would be drawn to a place like Arena Stage in DC because the ensemble there would give them continuity and a sustaining power. But New York is like the ultimate free market. You're here because you want to work with all of these different, interesting directors. Why would you want to settle down in a company and make yourself exclusive? So the Usual Suspects was about developing a loose sense of affiliation: creating a place you can call home, saying 'We're here for you. We have this menu of options of how we can work together. We have space we can give you. We call you ours, you can call us yours, but there's no obligation.' And we've been doing these summer retreats that are pretty critical for us and for our community, where we get people out of the city. By removing people from daily life we have been able to create something very pure, very Zen like.

Well, to go back to your thing about being a minister, it sounds like there is a spiritual aspect to this that fits with that?

I've never thought about that, but absolutely. What all our artists say when they have gone through this is that when they leave they feel renewed they feel recommitted to their art. Because I think what happens here in New York City is that you become so focused on being the entrepreneur that you have to be in order to survive here. What the retreat does is help you say: 'Well, I can't be an entrepreneur if I'm not first an artist.'

How do you identify the artists you are most interested in? What draws you to particular artist or to a particular project when you're programming?

It's interesting, right now we're in the middle of a conversation with some branding consultants. We're trying to figure out: what is our messaging? How can we best communicate with audiences, artists, funders and so on? We have been trying to find a catchphrase to describe ourselves, and one suggestion was 'brace for impact'. But that didn't sit well with me at all. Because it feels to me like the kind of play that I go to and really despise – one which sets out to manipulate your emotions. For me, the impact should be about trying to give you tools as an audience member to transform or to change – to sustain or nurture yourself in some way. The emotion has to be part of a wider process of trying to get somewhere. This place is a workshop not just for the artist but for you as an audience member to come and work on yourself.

So the word 'workshop' becomes a very active part of the name of the company, rather than just something you've inherited?

Yes. So I think the artists who interest me are the ones who work towards that goal and who have something bigger in their sights. We have this 2050 fellows programme, which is for emerging writers and directors. We have six of them for a year in residence.

Why is it called 2050?

It refers to the year 2050. It got named that because I was looking at some materials from the federal government census bureau that predicts that by the year 2050, Caucasians will still be the largest ethnic group of the population, but they will no longer be a majority. The fellowship used to be called Emerging Artists of Colour, but we decided that that was a little bit limiting and old school – not least because we also wanted to include trans people and deaf people and so on. Also many of the artists of colour felt very ambiguously about being labelled that way. So when I came across this statistic it felt right. It's about looking for a generation that's writing the future into existence or directing the future into existence. In my first meeting I have with any of them, I always say: 'You're an artist and you have a gift. Do you think that the first priority is to write, or create for yourself, or is it to write or create for someone else?'

And are you looking for a specific answer to that?

Generally, these are people who are early on in their practice and so they're very concerned with asking: 'Who am I?' Their creativity is about self-expression. What I always try to suggest to them is that: as you grow and mature, in one respect what you do is always going to be about you, but ultimately, what you do has to be about 'them' if you're going to fit in here. Art is about what the viewer, or the person who is experiencing it, gains from it.

This is another distinction, I think, in relation to that word: 'impact'. Are you doing this just to manipulate people? Or do you do it because you want them to get something from you? Is it a generous act, or is it a selfish act? Generally we're interested in looking for that generosity. We are always trying to find the joyful part, the fun part of something. When we're composing a season, we struggle with the question: 'Where is the fun in this?' This goes way back to Jean and Stephen. When they were conceiving this place in the 1970s and 1980s, there was a vital downtown theatre and then there was the uptown theatre. Uptown roughly corresponded to the commercial theatre and then the downtown theatre was sort of rebelling against that. What they observed at that time, and I was totally on board with this, was that the downtown world, in its zeal to reject the understood theatrical forms and experiences and to try to find new ways of doing things, almost always sacrificed content or ideas to the formal experiment.

Do you think that then made the work feel closed off to a lot of audiences?
Yes. Of course, I don't know that the people who were practising it would believe that, but I believe that and so did Stephen and Jean. And they articulated the issue by saying that they were interested in trying to keep pushing things formally but not at the cost of ideas and content – of substance or sustenance. When I got here, that made me feel like I was in the right place.

We're currently living through a very brutal political moment with Brexit in the UK and Trump in the United States. And I can see that you've got a Make America Gay Again baseball cap on your desk. So can you say something about the role of theatre within the context of political activism?
The end point and the starting point of activism and making art are different. I think they're both essential to a world transforming itself. And I do think people tend to have a propensity, or a gift on one side of that equation, or the other. I think it's really important for every individual to find their voice, wherever it may land. I think the difficult part is when a gifted, talented artist decides that making art isn't enough – writing a play isn't enough and that they believe that they have to man the barricades literally. They can then become a mediocre activist when they were a genius artist or vice versa. Activism by definition requires a clarity of vision that sees: these are the good guys and those are the bad guys; this is right and that is wrong and we're going to fix it. In order to strategize properly, you have to have that kind of clarity. I think on the artistic side, there is the opposite pursuit. The artists are trying to figure out which questions are the right ones to ask.

Yes. Outside of Hollywood movies good guys and bad guys don't make good stories. I always think you need to find the good guy and the bad guy within the *same* person. It's that dynamic, that internal conflict or ambiguity that drives the story.
Absolutely, I couldn't say it better. It has to be about complexity and contradiction. I actually believe that the most important purpose of art is to help us as individuals make our way through a world that is nothing but a paradox. I define a paradox as something that allows for there to be equal truths existing in complete conflict.

For me, the most powerful theatrical experiences are when I come out feeling: 'Yup that's the right question.' I don't generally respond to someone who's answering the question. Or if we do present someone who's giving an answer, it is in the context of saying: 'Here's one answer. What's yours?' We are giving you this answer to provoke you to think about what your individual answer is.

You've spoken so passionately about the influence that Joe and Zelda have had on you. Who are the other artistic directors whom you admire?
I think David Lan has done really wonderful things at the Young Vic. Mia Yoo across the street at La Mama is wonderful – she had this very particular task of taking over after the founder of this world-renowned organization and making it her own. I think Bob Falls has made quite a journey as an artistic leader – I've watched him for decades in Chicago. Bill Rauch at the Oregan Shakespeare Festival has maybe the most vivid example of a really diverse and inclusive theatre practice: with Shakespeare and contemporary work all mixed together and a big company of actors. It's like a lab for the future of what theatres have to be. I also greatly admire Sara Benson at Soho Rep and André Bishop at the Lincoln Center. He had a real challenge to make that place fly and I think he's done that in a very particular way. I think the work is excellent despite being for a very conservative audience. But I feel incredible admiration and respect to anybody who's willing to try and do this job. It's a really interesting thing because it has to be very personal but it absolutely cannot be about your ego.

12
RUFUS NORRIS

Rufus Norris became Director of the National Theatre in 2015. Situated on London's South Bank, the National Theatre produces a year round repertoire of classic plays, new work and musicals. It has three main auditoria: the Dorfman (capacity approximately 400), the Lyttelton (capacity 890) and the Olivier (capacity 1,160). It regularly tours nationally and internationally as well as taking work to the West End and Broadway.

Tell me about your journey to becoming Director of the National Theatre.

I trained as an actor at RADA, although I didn't ever actually want to be an actor. That sounds odd, but it's just that I didn't want to go to university. Rather, I wanted something which was going to keep me occupied – which would keep me from being bored and keep me from being a more boring version of myself. The great thing about acting is that you've really got to be in the present moment – you have to use all of yourself – so I wanted that as a training. I then worked as an actor on and off for about three or four years while doing other things to earn money as well including working in the building trade and writing a lot of music.

I met a guy called Brian Astbury who had, in the past, set up a theatre called The Space in Cape Town with Athol Fugard and Yvonne Bryceland – which was an equivalent venue to the Market Theatre in Johannesburg. But they, like many liberal white South Africans at that time, had come to the UK. He was always encouraging emerging actors to make their own work rather than just hanging around waiting for stuff to come along. He was setting up this new venue in Paddington and he asked me to be in a play that he was directing there. I think his ulterior motive was that he wanted me to get involved with building the theatre itself – because he knew that I knew all about putting up stud walls and that kind of stuff. So we did that, and we built this theatre called Arts Threshold.

The play was called *The Fisherman's Ring* and I remember the writer came to see the first performance and fell asleep because it was massively overlong. I had to be naked in this thankless show, and it felt like a real message, from God or whoever, to me to say: 'stop acting'! But at the same time, a friend of mine, Deirdre Strath, had written a script called *The Lizzie Play*, which I just happened to read on the tube one day, and I thought it was absolutely fantastic. So I went into Arts Threshold the next day, and said: 'I've got a play that I think we should try and do. Maybe I could write the music for it, or maybe I could be in it.' And Brian said: 'Or maybe you could direct it.' So I did. And from the first day of rehearsal, I knew that that was it. I'd found the thing that I wanted to do. So I went on to direct another three or four shows at Arts Threshold. I did some assisting at Theatr Clwyd under Helena Kaut-Howson and set up some tours of shows with friends and so on.

I then took over at Arts Threshold and ran it for two or three years. It had absolutely no funding. Each show had a budget of £150 and we relied entirely on the box office income, which went up and down. So it was a learning curve. We produced twelve shows a year. The actors who performed in the evening cleaned the theatre before they performed, while the actors who had rehearsed there in the day ran the cafe and the box office in the evening. So it was a very socialist enterprise. We became experts at how to unblock the plumbing in the loos and we'd go into hotels to steal toilet paper because we couldn't afford it! No one got paid anything. I was on the dole pretty much non-stop from about 1989 until about 1996. I'd do the odd acting or directing job and I'd come off it for a while then go back on. But still, I was working 100 hours a week for that whole time. It was a different form of subsidy then – I don't know how people get through that crucial period now.

I then started freelancing. I directed some drama school shows and did a show at the Gate Theatre. I formed my own company called Wink with the designer Katrina Lindsay and the lighting designer Natasha Chivers. We did two or three national tours and did some stuff at the Young Vic studio in the days when Tim Supple was running it. To fund it we'd have parties or do beer runs to France where we'd buy beer and then sell it here – anything to get a bit of money.

Then, in 1995, my partner got pregnant. So I thought: 'Okay. I need to earn a living.' At that point I'd never really been involved with any of the big theatres like the National or the Royal Court. I had never felt included in that whole network of happening young directors. But I'd just been to see a show at the Court, *Some Voices* by Joe Penhall, which was directed by Ian Rickson – this was before he became artistic director there. I wrote to him and said how great I thought it was and so he agreed to meet me. He suggested I apply to do one of the Court's residencies, which I then got, and so I spent a brilliant year there. I was sharing an office with Stephen Daldry, James Macdonald, Ian Rickson and Indhu Rubasingham. And David Lan was their literary associate at that point. The script meetings at the Royal Court were my university in a way – listening to Max Stafford-Clark, Graham Whybrow, the literary manager at the time, and Elyse Dodgeson and so on.

Soon after that, David Lan took over the Young Vic and started to really focus on directors, and eventually, I became his associate. I had a deep love affair with that theatre and I got very close with David who, after Brian Astbury, became my main mentor. It's been amazing watching him run that place – seeing his focus on the projects that he's produced and the way that, over eighteen years, he's been kind of like an ironmonger who has wrought it into the unique identity that it has now. And I made a lot of work there under his guidance.

After several years, I went back to freelancing. I started making films and started working at the National where I did two or three shows, including the musical *London Road*. That was really crucial – partly because it went really well but also because it was about community, and it made me realize that I really missed that. So I mentioned to Sebastian Born, the NT's literary manager, that I would love to be more involved. Within a couple of weeks, Nick Hytner called me and said: 'Would you like to come and join us as an associate?' I really wasn't expecting that, but it was a no-brainer, though I'm completely different from Nick. In some ways, we have nothing in common at all, though there is a fair amount of mutual respect. I was an associate for him for three years or so.

Then he announced he was going to leave. I didn't think about applying until one or two people started encouraging me to think about it. So my partner Tanya and I had a series of discussions about it. And eventually, she said: 'What's the film that you'll do in the next five years that will make you think "I'm really glad I didn't apply for the National?"' And there wasn't one, so I decided to go for it and I got it and that is when the learning began.

It can be a really tough job at times. But I was talking to Vicky Heywood the other night about her time as executive director at the RSC alongside Michael Boyd. And she was saying that there was a moment eight or nine years in where Michael said to her: 'You know what? If we ever start to think we are bulletproof, then that will mean it's probably time to go.'

The National is a massive building – both in terms of its physical size, with three large auditoria, but also in the fact that it has a national remit. How do you go about managing something of that scale?

The simple answer is it's completely overwhelming. In terms of the scale of the building, the experts tell us that the maximum number you can have in proper community is 150. Well, we've got around 1,500 staff here. They're working across three theatres and we have six, seven, eight shows in the building at any one time, with another 150 being cooked up. So it can start to feel a bit anonymous and that doesn't suit everyone. Some people much prefer to be in a small team. But that's just the nature of the organization. And even though we're big, it can be very easy to become overambitious. You might say, one day: 'It'd be great if we did this', and people will start running off trying to make that happen. But the next day you might go: 'Or we could do that', and very quickly, you find that you have capacity issues and a lack of focus.

You can't do everything, so to make the right decisions you have to really listen to the people around you and not pretend that you know more about this stuff than you actually do just because you've got the top job. And the brilliant thing about the National is that it's stuffed full of brilliant people. That is one thing that that level of subsidy, that reputation and that demand for quality can bring. We have to have, in theatre terms, the best director of development, the best director of marketing and so on. Our chief operating officer, Liz Fosbury, is absolutely formidable. It's great watching her jousting with our chair at board meetings – they are both people who really understand numbers in a way that I never will. But I can now read what's going on, and how they're second-guessing and playing games with each other to make sure that she's got what she needs to deliver the budget on target next year, and he's got what he needs to make sure that the reserves are getting built up. These are people who are really good at what they do. So if I were to suddenly fall over, the machine wouldn't drop a beat. It would just keep going and would probably be able to do so for quite a long time. My job is about making sure that I am constantly communicating with those brilliant staff and that I keep them feeling involved. I have to make sure I listen to them so that I'm making the right decisions.

Another thing I have come to understand, at a personal level, is that burnout is a real thing – that was one big lesson for me when I started. I directed too much in the first couple of years, and I'm pretty good when it comes to stamina, but there's a limit.

You have to manage a lot of very senior artists who have worked here for many years. Did you ever find resistance from them when you took over in terms of the changes you wanted to make?

It's probably the case that the people whom I've had the most challenge from have been my contemporaries, not the younger ones and not the older ones. But at the same time, the people I've had the best time with have also been my contemporaries because we've known each other for such a long time, and we can be straight with each other. But in terms of those very senior people, take David Hare, for example. He is a man who doesn't suffer fools. He is very opinionated, very outspoken. But he's also the first person to say: 'Rufus, I need some producing on this show. Can you get involved with this?' Which is great – any fear I had about treading on his toes was misplaced. He would say: 'No, do your job.' And when I've had to have a toe-to-toe with him about marketing or whatever it is, in the end he will say: 'I think I'm being told a definitive here. Right. On we go.' But of course there have been some really tricky occasions and there will be many more, no doubt. It's just the nature of it. The only way for me to avoid that is to not work with challenging people, but I really wouldn't be doing my job if that were the case.

And how do you go about forming a coherent vision or artistic policy for such a large building?

It's a given that the work has got to be high quality. But beyond that, the policy has to start with the name of the building. It is called the National, so the place should represent the whole country, and it should also represent the city that we are based in. So the policy has to be about breadth: breadth of artists and breadth of audience. We have to make sure that we're a broad church when it comes to taste.

A key thing for me is that we have to have proper representation on stage and proper representation through the staff. For example, in the Dorfman we recently opened *The Great Wave* – a play with ten East Asian actors telling a story about Japan and North Korea. It's had great press and people have really responded to the deep humanity in the story and the honesty of the playing of it. At the same time, we've got Bryan Cranston performing in *Network* at the Lyttelton. The thing about Bryan is that he brings in a load of people who don't go to the theatre but who do watch *Breaking Bad*. Many of those people have never been into a theatre at all, let alone into the National Theatre. So it's really great seeing the number of first-time visitors he's attracting and then what that does to the age and diversity of our audience.

But fundamentally, we have to really grapple with the fact that even though we like to think that we are very liberal and open-minded, we're actually quite a closed shop in lots of ways. So to address that, we've put in place targets to increase our diversity. For instance, we're saying that 50 per cent of our directors should be female by 2021. Anyone who says that will reduce quality is basically saying that men are inherently better directors than women and that's bullshit. What we're talking about is representation. Thirteen per cent of the people in the country as a whole are BAME and 40 per cent of the people in London are BAME. So we set a target for 20 per cent of writers and directors to be BAME, and then a minimum of 25 per cent of people on stage to be so. Now those are really hard targets to hit because theatre has not historically presented itself as a community into which certain people are welcome. It can be quite self-selective. If you're a young British person whose parents come from Somalia, there is little in the theatre world that says to you: 'You can have a career.'

As Director of the National Theatre, do you feel that a significant part of your role involves being a public figure and advocate?

The advocacy side of it is very important. But it's very hard to speak as the voice of theatre until people respect you, and people won't respect you until you've earned it. There's no shortcut for that. I feel this year I've done my first bit of public advocacy in relation to arts in education and that's hopefully the tip of a growing iceberg. But you can't just write something off the cuff. You've got to back it up through communication and lots of listening. In the case of that issue, I've had lots of meetings with head teachers and have been really focused on bringing the learning department into the centre of what we do.

One of the frustrating things about arts education is that you really get the sense that our education policy since Michael Gove was in charge, and probably before, has been driven by personal experience and dogma. You listen to Jeremy Corbyn and Theresa May arguing about grammar schools, and she will say: 'Jeremy, Jeremy, we both went to good grammar schools.' And you think: 'Well, what the hell has that got to do with anything?' When you're talking about defence policy, you don't talk about the little toy tanks that you played with as a kid. You talk to generals who really understand what it's like in the field. And in education, you should be talking to education experts, to economists, to people who can see how the world is developing, not just thinking about where you personally went.

But ultimately, it's about finding a balance between ego and humility all the time. I have a platform, but I've got to be really careful about when I choose to use it, and I have to make sure that what I say is informed. This is especially the case in an environment where we've got a kind of new conservatism coming in and a lot of people are fearful and resentful which is made worse by the rise of right-leaning commentary on social media and in mainstream media too. It's been interesting for my generation of people in the arts to discover that we are distrusted and disliked by many others.

You mean by the people on the other side of the divide over Brexit?

Yes – in terms of the way that we're perceived and the way that we're painted by some of the press. We're very easy targets. So you've got to make yourself a less easy target by making absolutely sure that you talk sense. So when it comes to talking about the arts in education, it's easy to say: 'Well, I think it's really good for kids to have the capacity for creative self-expression.' I believe that passionately. But until you can back it up with data, you get patronized and ignored. What you can say is that the creative industries are the second fastest growing industry sector in this country – bringing in £92 billion a year. So financially it's really easy to make the argument that if you don't have a creative greenhouse in our education sector, then what's going to happen? Where's the next Jony Ive going to come from? He's the chief design officer at Apple and he went to a polytechnic in Newcastle. He's just a Brit who happens to be running the world, and there are loads of people like that who, like me, had access to art when they came through their education.

Who are the artistic directors who have inspired you or mentored you?

Stephen Daldry was really important because of his fearlessness. I assisted him two or three times and was at the Royal Court when he was in charge. He had this great way of exploring an idea where he'd go: 'I want to do such and such. Tell me how to do it.' And you'd have to say something, and then he'd go: 'No, not that. Give me something else.' And he'd keep asking for something else until you'd come up with something and he'd ask: 'Where's that going?' He'd start pulling on this bit of string that you'd come up with and where you didn't even know yourself where it was going until you got to the end of it. And then he might say 'right'. Meaning, 'That's the extent of the idea that you've just had and I don't want it. But it's led me to this piece of string that I do want so thank you very much'. 'And then you'd realize that you'd helped somebody who was in a position to make decisions and he really had listened so it had been a real collaboration. And I admire David Lan for his politics, his dramaturgical skill and his absolute focus. I owe him a huge amount for his guidance, passion and example.

More recently I've come to admire Oskar Eustis at the Public. I'm really inspired by what they do with their Public Works programme, their music lab and the way that they develop work. We've formed quite a strong personal friendship very quickly. By comparison to him, I'm a total beginner. But you could fit all five of the theatres at the Public into the Olivier. So we have really different models. But when I walk into that theatre, that's where I want to be.

There are lots of my contemporaries who are doing great work. Indhu Rubasingham is a great mate. She's had a couple of real battles at Kiln but it's been good to watch her ride them out. And I think seeing how front-foot Vicky Featherstone was last year in relation to all the sexual harassment stuff was very impressive. Rupert Goold is somebody I've completely grown up with. He has totally reimagined what the Almeida can be and has done it very well. Josie Rourke broke real ground at the Donmar in forging a way for female artistic directors. Kwame getting the Young Vic now is really exciting, and I'll do whatever I can to support that because it's really important that it goes well. And Ian Rickson and Dominic Cooke both brought very different qualities to the Royal Court. It was very interesting watching Dom go through that and seeing him literally turn grey and then escape and become completely demob happy! And I've benefited from that by saying: 'Okay, come and be an associate here. Come and turn my desk over.' He's a brilliant associate. And then there are directors who inspire me like Marianne Elliot, Simon McBurney and Robert LePage.

Though arguably the most inspiring theatre leader whom this country's thrown up in the last decade is Sonia Friedman. As a commercial producer she works on a completely different model to us, but look at the health of London theatre and look at the shows which are doing well and how many of them are Sonia's.

Richard Eyre said in his diaries that the key thing an artistic director has to do is to be able to take joy in other people's success.

There's a lot of inspiration to be had if you look around and can get over your defensiveness about other people's success. Absolutely. I remember going to a party at the National Theatre Studio a million years ago and Nick Hytner gave a speech, where he said: 'What's good for General Motors is good for the United States.' And what he meant was that what is good for theatre as a whole is good for the National Theatre. So if the Old Vic's *Girl from the North Country* and if *Hamilton* are making London a great place to come to, then that's fantastic. It's great for the National because we all drag each other up.

13
DIANE PAULUS

Diane Paulus has been artistic director of the American Repertory Theater (A.R.T.) at Harvard University since 2008. The A.R.T. produces a mixed repertoire of new American plays, classic plays and musicals in its 556-seat auditorium. It also runs a club theatre venue called Oberon, as well producing in other spaces throughout Boston and on tour nationally and internationally. Its mission is to 'expand the boundaries of theatre'.

Could you tell me about your journey to running the A.R.T.?
I grew up in New York City, born and raised near Lincoln Center – that was my backyard. I did a lot of dance as a child – dancing with the New York City Ballet. I also played piano for ten years, and alongside that I was doing theatre. But when I went to Harvard as an undergrad I initially wanted to pursue politics. Growing up in the 1970s in New York I didn't understand why the city couldn't be a better place for more people to live. At that time it was rough; it bears no resemblance to how it is now. I had this dream of being the mayor of New York.

But I did a lot of extracurricular theatre while I was taking classes in government. And I developed this clarity that the arts was something I wanted to pursue. That was where I felt the most alive, and where I felt the impossible was possible. I wrote my senior thesis on Judith Beck and Julian Malina's company The Living Theatre. There was no theatre major at Harvard, so I was doing this within the Social Studies department, under the guise of social anthropology. As part of that, I interviewed Robert Brustein, founder of the A.R.T. I was a 21-year-old senior at Harvard sitting there in his office. At the time, I never thought that that would eventually become my office!

When I left Harvard I went to a new acting school in New York called the New Actors Workshop that had been founded by Mike Nichols, Paul Sills and George Morrison. Two really important mentors emerged for me out of that experience. The first was Paul Sills, the son of Viola Spolin who was the founder of the improvisational 'Theatre Games' movement in the United States. She worked with immigrant children at the turn of the century and wrote a book called *Improvisation for the Theatre,* which is kind of the bible of that movement. Paul took these games and put them into a professional theatre context, which eventually led to the creation of The Second City[1] in Chicago. The second was Mike Nichols, who would teach scene study masterclasses. We spent four hours every Wednesday night in the studio with Mike bringing in scenes from Aeschylus, Neil Simon, Tennessee Williams, whoever. He would talk to us, as actors, about every aspect of the work. And because there were no directors, we would choose how to edit the scene, how to stage it and what props to use. We were making all these directorial choices even though we were actors, and that was huge for me. It gave me a lot of the tools I now use in directing – though I didn't realize that at the time.

When it was time to graduate from the programme, we were all taking about what we wanted to do. People were saying: 'I want to get an agent' or 'I want to go to Hollywood' or whatever. I kid you not, when it came around to me, I said: 'Well, I want to be Robert Brustein and run the American Repertory Theater.' And my classmates were like: 'What are you talking about?!' That place was so not on their radar. But I had just graduated from Harvard so I'd seen all the shows at the A.R.T. when I was there. I'd seen work by Robert Wilson, Philip Glass, Andrei Serban, Joanne Akalaitis, etc. I grew up in New York, but going to the A.R.T. had shown me a whole other form of theatre.

Out in the real world, I had no patience for the normal actor thing of just sitting around waiting for a job. My entrepreneurial instincts took over, and I started organizing my acting classmates into shows, which I would both act in and direct. I did *La Ronde* by Schnitzler in the studio at the school; I found an abandoned garden on the Upper West Side and directed *Twelfth Night*. Paul Sills had a farm in Door County, Wisconsin, and he said: 'Why don't you come to Wisconsin? Get out of the city?' So I raised the money, and I took graduates from the school out there, and we started a theatre company. And I spent the next five years in rural Wisconsin doing theatre – that was my experimental training ground.

---

[1]The Second City is an improvisational comedy venue which has launched the careers of many prominent comics including Bill Murray and Tina Fey.

Eventually, I felt I needed some more formal directing training. So I went to Columbia. This was 1997, and I studied with Anne Bogart and Andrei Serban, who were really important teachers for me. Upon graduation, I went right back to making theatre with a company, this time with Columbia graduates. One of the first shows we did was *The Donkey Show* in the lobby of Dodge Hall at Columbia School of the Arts. After a year of doing that show downtown for free in clubs and found spaces, the producer Jordan Roth took it formally to a place off-Broadway where it ran for six years, and then it played the Edinburgh Festival Fringe and went to London's Hanover Grand nightclub.

So I was making theatre in the trenches, and simultaneously I was starting to do work in opera because Andrei Serban had opened a door to that for me. I had this odd profile of being a downtown avant-garde kid who also did Monte Verde operas. I then got a job working for David Lan – directing an opera called *Lost Highway*, based on the David Lynch film, as part of an ENO/Young Vic collaboration. And it was when I was at the Young Vic that I got a phone call asking if i would be interested in throwing my hat in the ring for this job at the A.R.T.

I was freelancing a lot at this point – travelling around the United States and Europe. So when this offer came up, I thought two things. One, there aren't many theatres in the United States that I would uproot my life for and devote blood, sweat and tears to. I had known the A.R.T. since my college years, and it felt like the ultimate destination of my career in theatre. And I'd heard that it was struggling – the audience wasn't coming. I thought: 'If the A.R.T., with that amazing history and that potential energy that comes from being in a major intellectual urban centre, is dying, then what hope is there for anything?'

The second thing I thought had to do with the nature of being a freelance director. When you make a show in that context, you're invited to direct, but you're not really let into the big picture financially. You say what you want, and then you are told you have to cut things. You are never given a sense of what the total resources are for the production. How is all the money being spent? I remember on one show seeing a line item for a dress that was $6,000. I had come from making shows out of shopping bags of donated clothes, so I thought: 'That dress goes on stage for all of three minutes. Maybe let's not spend $6,000 on it!' You also have very little say in the marketing of a show. And I always felt that as an artist you spend so much time on the art side of things, but that's only half of the equation. The delivery system is the other half, and I wanted a say in that.

The A.R.T.'s mission statement was: 'The A.R.T. is dedicated to expanding the boundaries of theatre through classic works of the canon and the new works of tomorrow.' And when I read that I thought: 'Okay, now I really know that I can throw myself hook, line, and sinker into this theatre.' Because that mission is so expansive. Expanding the boundaries of theatre means asking: 'How do you produce it? Who's the audience? What is theatre?' That was everything that I had already been doing as a director: making work in different locations, working site-specifically, breaking the rules of programming, blending marketing with performance.

So how did the history of the theatre shape your approach to running it? Presumably the fact that it was in crisis had a big impact?

Yes. There's always that question of what kind of theatre you would rather inherit. One that's doing brilliantly or one that's broken? There are advantages to both. I inherited a theatre that was going through a crisis with its audience – capacity was down. Shows were playing to houses of 50 or 60 per cent or less. And I think Harvard was looking at that situation and thinking: 'Why are we carrying this?' I knew that my task was not to go to Harvard with my hands out to say: 'I need more money.' It was to make the theatre the most vibrant hub on campus. If I could get everyone clamouring for seats, and if I could get both faculty and students there, and if it could be the most sought-after night out on Harvard's campus, then we would find people who would support the theatre financially.

So I came to the interview with very populist ideas. I talked a lot about the audience because the audience is what inspires everything I do as a director. I never think of the audience as a polluting thing or something that is distracting. And that is a very different perspective from some of the attitudes we see around culture in the United States. I think many artists grew hardened over the course of the twentieth century and came to believe that audiences don't understand what they want or need. They came to believe that people wouldn't buy it or pay for it of their own accord, so we had to subsidize it and give it to them like a vitamin shot, as if it was something that was good for them.

But I want people to *want* to go to the theatre. I want to reach a broader audience. And because A.R.T. is in a university town, you have a lot of young people and a lot of people who are changing the world through diplomacy, law, social media and so on. I knew that if I could get them engaged, it would be a test of: Can the theatre play a more central role in who we are as citizens? Forget making good art – to this day, that is really not what drives me. Rather, I want to ask: 'What are the issues that we're grappling with? What do we need to talk about? Who are the artists that are going to make the most noise and catalyse a discussion?'

When I'm programming, I always ask: 'What are the ideas in the show, and how are they affecting a dialogue that we need to have?' It's this question that led us to create a programme we call 'Act II', in which we curate what happens after the show. Every theatre has post-performance discussions, where some expert comes out to explain the show to the audience. But I just felt that form was dead. I've always believed that what happens in that precious thirty minutes after the show is as important as the show itself. So I thought: 'Can't we just take that transformative moment and extend it at the theatre?'

We began this experiment with a production of *Prometheus Bound*. This was a crazy new rock musical version of the Aeschylus story about tyranny. It took place on our second stage, where the audience stood and all the action happened around them. We partnered with Amnesty International because we felt that *Prometheus Bound* was the first play about a prisoner of conscience. And we dedicated every week to a different prisoner of conscience around the world. At the end of the show, actors would read aloud about a case, and then a whole corps of Amnesty volunteers would emerge from the crowd and invite the audience to stay and sign postcards and take action. It was a huge success. It galvanized the theatre, brought new people in and made social engagement happen.

So as an artistic institutional leader, I have to look at everything that surrounds what happens on our stage. What does the lobby look like? What's the feeling in the building? You have to shift the whole way an institution thinks about the event.

What draws you to a particular project or artist when you're programming? How do you put a season together?

We look to develop projects that are taking the theatre form and pushing it. That can be either mean pushing things in terms of structure and ideas, or it can be in relation to the kind of artists that we're bringing to the table: people who've never worked in the theatre before. I often think: 'What show will create noise? What show will vibrate beyond just being a show?' And that can come through artists who have a specific vision for a particular subject matter. But it can also come from bringing artists together to combust with a certain subject – through a development process that we call the Roundtable. For instance, the Harvard University Center for the Environment (HUCE) came to me saying: 'No one's listening. We have to do something together.' So we brought climate scientists and experts from the centre around a table with artists: choreographers, playwrights, directors. And they talked and began to generate ideas together. And those initial conversations led to a multi-year partnership and multiple commissions supported by HUCE.

In my first couple of years, I felt like I had to run to get to each new season. But as of around three or four years ago, we've become able to start seeding projects on a three-year trajectory. And we've created courses at Harvard around the development of specific shows. When I did *Porgy and Bess*, I taught a course on that production with a culture scholar at Harvard named Marjorie Garber. We taught the course in real time with the development of the show. We were reading the novel, the play, the opera and watching the film. Then the students were looking at the development of our version and bringing in their own ideas about what this show means today.

Before we started this interview, you mentioned to me that you were probably the only woman of colour who runs a League of Resident Theatres (LORT) venue. Is that something you feel especially conscious of? How do you approach the wider questions around diversity and inclusion?

The stats on women who have leadership roles in LORT Theatres are depressing. Women make up only around 20 per cent of artistic directors, and that hasn't changed in twenty years. What was interesting in this LORT study is that it showed that more women are leading the mid-management departments, but they are not rising to the top. So we need to do a lot of work there.

I think for most theatres, the first place they are able to achieve diversity is on the stage. It becomes a whole other situation with staff, where often you have people in long-term jobs. But the hardest place is on the board because you're under pressure at a not-for-profit to really lean on them to give financially. Your priority when looking for board members is, who can write the biggest check. That is no doubt important, but it can't be the only priority; otherwise you may not have as diverse a board as you need. There is no question that this is a big issue. It's an issue that is facing the whole of the United States. The demographics of this country are changing, and our artistic institutions need to change to reflect that.

How do you see your role when it comes to developing and producing the work of other directors?

My job is to ensure that the process is maximal for them. People come to us because they want their shows to be developed. So we invite directors and writers to the table to read their work and get aggressive feedback and go through our dramaturgical engine. I keep my eye on everything that has to do with that process: the script, the selection of the artists, the design of the show and the conversation about audience and community engagement. I attend run-throughs, watch the dress rehearsals and give notes throughout all those landmark points.

I learnt something I will never forget when I was working on *Hair* at The Public. We had an extraordinarily tight schedule, and The Public's artistic director, Oskar Eustis, who is one of my mentors, came to me and he said: 'Every department's going to come and say, "My needs are the most important." But don't get pulled around by all of that. You have to decide what's important.' So an artistic director is like a senior executive coach who helps you to keep your eye on the prize and the priorities. I feel that especially when I watch a show that's in dress and previews. I have to help identify what must be fixed and help artists through the process of making those big changes.

The world is going through a very particular political moment currently, with Trump in the United States and Brexit in the UK. What role, if any, do you see theatre as having in relation to wider political events?

I think we have a huge role to play as another space for people to listen, to learn and to understand what's happening in our country. We're inundated with information, and it's overwhelming: We are living in a media-saturated age that provides information whenever we want it; we can access crisis at any moment. Just take out your device from your pocket, scroll and scroll, and you can consume ever more tragedy and outrage. And yet, in the process, too often we end up feeling numb and isolated. It becomes a vicious circle.

I also think it is important that we don't become another echo chamber. The day after the election, I just felt like I had failed – that, as an artistic leader, I had not done my job of listening properly. I thought: 'What happened? I guess everybody else feels this way, and I don't, and I am just in my own little lonely bubble.' So we have to provide a space in which we can penetrate to a deeper dialogue on these issues. I think we've lost a sense of our democracy, and theatre can play a role in changing that. But that means we have to open up our theatres. We cannot be elite. If we're all just patting ourselves on the back for our willingness to listen to certain things and not others, then we're not really participating in democracy. So a question I've been thinking about a lot is: how do we do that?

What do you think the answer to that might be?

I really don't know. The challenge is: how do we bring different narratives to the stage that are not just the narratives we want to hear? When Anna Deavere Smith came to the A.R.T. with *Notes from the Field* – a show about mass incarceration in the United States, police brutality and race relations – I thought: 'Okay, we're in a liberal bubble in Cambridge. Everybody's going to get the show.' But I was so surprised by how many audience members who lived down the block from the theatre were uncomfortable with the show or didn't want to talk about it, or didn't think it related to them. I think, as much as we say: 'We all get it', we don't.

On the other hand, I have seen the toll that the times we are living in have taken on my staff over the last six months. Life in the theatre is hard – everybody's overworked and underpaid, and there is the added burden right now of the current political climate. So how do we function and do our part within that? Sometimes I feel like we should just make shows that make people happy to come to the theatre. I think: 'Maybe we shouldn't do anything about politics and just let people come to the theatre and have a catharsis of another nature.'

Who are the artistic directors who have inspired you?
Anne Bogart is such an important artistic leader in the United States. She was my graduate school teacher and is a huge inspiration for me. And, of course, there is Oskar Eustis and David Lan. When we were about to undertake a big capital campaign project, the first people I went to were David and Oscar. And I'm about to bring a show to Manhattan Theatre Club for the first time. I've never worked for Lynn Meadow before, but I'm really excited because she's the founder of this long-established theatre and is a woman leader. And, of course, what Bob Brustein did when he set up the A.R.T. was absolutely seminal for me – both as an artist in my own right and as the person who is now the leader of that theatre.

Being an artistic director can be a somewhat lonely experience because you're so busy doing work in your own building. So it's great when there are moments where you can reach out and connect. James Bundy at Yale Rep has been a great colleague in that regard. But I think Bill Rauch at the Oregon Shakespeare Festival is my biggest soulmate as an artistic director. Whenever I'm having a problem I just say: 'What would Bill do? Let me go talk to Bill.' I think we're maybe of a certain generation together that made theatre in the trenches for so many years. We both have a spirit of populism and an interest in asking: 'What is that populist impulse, and how can we make that work?'

14
JOSIE ROURKE

Josie Rourke was artistic director of the Bush Theatre from 2008 to 2012. She then became artistic director of the Donmar Warehouse which she ran until 2018. The Donmar is a 251-seat theatre in Covent Garden which produces a mixed repertoire of classic plays and new work.

Tell me about your journey through running first the Bush Theatre and then the Donmar Warehouse.

I was twenty-nine when I got the Bush job. In truth, I applied for it because I was just sort of pissed off. I had done two very critically successful shows at the RSC. And I think in my head I was living in some kind of Stratford-upon-Avon-style idyll where I thought I would do a show for the RSC every year, do some other freelancing on the side, and just be content working my way through Shakespeare. But then I didn't get offered another job there! So I thought, rather impulsively: 'Sod this. I can't be sitting on my hands waiting for stuff to happen. I should go and try and do something for myself. If I feel frustration, then I should act on that.'

The Bush appealed because I really wanted to run a new work building. I had an awareness of there being an unbelievable number of promising playwrights among my generation. And I could see a problem in the new writing culture that I wanted to do something about: essentially I wanted to get writers out of development and just produce them. The first thing I did at the Bush was to work out how to change the structure of how we commissioned and developed work so that we could just put plays on more directly. And that was an amazing four and a half years of my life in which we produced early plays by Lucy Kirkwood, Mike Bartlett, Jack Thorne, Nick Payne, James Graham and so on – the most amazing group of writers. It was a very fertile moment in playwriting.

I was drawn to the Donmar because I had a strong emotional attachment to the building having trained there under Sam Mendes. I had a great empathy with the space and what you could do with it. When I was appointed AD there, all of the reporting focused on the fact that I was the first woman artistic director of a major London theatre. But that's quite a fine distinction because you already had Jude Kelly at the Southbank – though the difference is that she's running a big arts centre and not necessarily directing work there. So I suppose what they meant by that was that I was the first woman who, in the British tradition, was a director as well as an artistic director. And having someone who does both of those things is relatively unique to our culture – for instance, you can't become artistic director of the National if you're not a star director. At least that is true at the moment, though that may change.

So all of the press around the Donmar was really about my gender. And one of the things that motivated me to apply was the feeling that, as a woman, I felt a certain responsibility to cut that path. I had a sense that if someone planted a flag in London, then hopefully that would lead to some of the changes that we were struggling to make. But truthfully, what felt more significant to me is that I was only thirty-four and so this became the first major London theatre to be taken over by someone of my generation. It was a big moment for me and my peers to go: 'We got the keys to one of these big buildings.'

Also, that was balanced with a desire to change the programme at the Donmar. Although this hasn't been particularly widely noticed or written about, one of the most significant things that we've been able to do in my time there is to dedicate space to thinking specifically about how directors were given opportunities to develop work. So we have been able to say to Lyndsey Turner: 'Come and have this encounter with Brian Friel' and she has now done three of his plays. Or we could say to Phyllida Lloyd after she did the all-female *Julius Caesar* – 'Look, it should be a trilogy of shows.' That actually felt particularly profound. It's easy to forget, given the pace of change in equality over the past five years, but some of the reviews of *Julius Caesar* were really horrible about the fact that it was an all-female production. I remember the *Telegraph* using that awful Doctor Johnson quote saying: 'A woman preaching is like a dog walking on his hind legs. It is not done well; but you are surprised to find it done at all.'

So there was this violent reaction to that production. But to have the power as an artistic director to be able to say to that director: 'And now you should make two more,' was enormously important. So the encounters with directors where you're actually trying to allow a degree of authorship to them over the plays they do and the way in which they do them have been hugely significant. On the whole, I spent my time at the Bush thinking about writing and my time at the Donmar thinking about directing.

Alongside championing those writers, there are two other things that characterized your time at the Bush, one was facing down the Arts Council when they tried to make a huge cut to the theatre's funding, and the other was moving the Bush into its new building. Can you say a little more about those two very institutional aspects of running a building? Did those things inform your artistic programming, or did they just feel like millstones that needed to be carried?

It's a weird thing when you're an artistic director that people on the outside of it often talk about it as being a 'weight' or a 'burden' – they use all these heavy metaphors. Actually, my experience from the inside is that it's sort of light and quick. It's such a dynamic world that when crises occur, it's like your playing a kind of crazy racket sport with all the stuff that's going on, as much as you are putting your shoulder to something and pushing. The Arts Council stuff was like that. They announced these bizarre cuts to our funding but they wouldn't tell us why. I was less than six months into the job and I really knew very little about what I was doing. I called a couple of other artistic directors and quite a few said: 'Sorry. It's game over. Bad luck. But don't worry, you can come do a show for me after you close.'

Is that how serious a threat the cut was?

Yes. It was a big cut – around 40 per cent. And bear in mind at that point the Bush was a tiny venue – so the box office revenue was minuscule. We did some trust and foundation fundraising but not very much and we only raised a small amount from private individuals. The model for theatre funding in London tends to be done in thirds – a third of your money comes from public subsidy, a third from box office and a third from fundraising. But the Bush didn't have the balance to sustain it in that kind of crisis. It's like being a small business in that sense. If you have three clients and one of your clients goes away, you hope you can rely on your other two clients enough that you won't go under. We couldn't do that. For me, the main panic, aside from my commitments to the writers and their plays and the value of that institution itself, was thinking: 'I've just met these people on the staff and we're going to have to make them redundant.'

So I did a kind of amateurish girl detective-style request under the Freedom of Information Act. And I put the Arts Council under enormous pressure to try to deliver that paperwork in time for us to respond to the recommended cut – this was just before Christmas. I think I honestly thought that if they didn't do it in time, I could probably get some kind of judicial review. Anyway, I put them under slightly too much pressure and they delivered it the night before that now infamous meeting at the Young Vic that Equity organized with Peter Hewitt, the then chief executive of the Arts Council. I remember people at that meeting were speaking out very emotionally and viscerally about how wrong they felt the funding decisions that the Arts Council had made were. And I stood up in that room, with adrenaline coursing through my body – the thing I was mainly aware of was my leg shaking – and I said: 'We made a Freedom of Information request, and the following documents were delivered to the Bush Theatre last night. Among other discrepancies, they appear to mis-record our audience figures by quite a significant percentage.' And I then said: 'Do you not think we should call a halt to all of this and perform a full public audit?' That was what really made them panic.

So that was quite a big deal. And I can probably talk about this now because it's far enough in the past, but we went to the Arts Council for a meeting and they pulled out an Excel spreadsheet, which had our audience figures in it that were correctly recorded, and I reached into the pack of FOI documents and pulled out a corresponding Excel spreadsheet, which was identical except for the fact that the figures were different in it. At which point I said: 'I think you better give us our funding back now!'

In retrospect, I came to understand that their decision had been linked to a plan by the theatre's board to move the Bush into a new building that would be in the heart of a commercial business park next to Riverside Studios in Hammersmith. The board had never really made their plans for this clear to me and I thought it was kind of a bonkers idea anyway and had asked the Arts Council to give me time to look into it. But when you looked through all of the emails that had come to us through the FOI, it was clear that the Arts Council had, on the basis of those plans, which they thought were a bad idea, already decided to cut the funding. The problem with this is that they hadn't communicated that to the board. They hadn't said: 'Listen, your funding will be jeopardized if you do this.'

So when they did, eventually, restore our funding, I had an off-the-record conversation where they said: 'You've got one funding agreement. You've got three years. If at the end of that three years you've not found a new building, that's it.' So that was quite a clear egg timer! And we were then able to say the Hammersmith and Fulham Council: 'If you don't help us get a new building, you will lose us completely,' and I could say to the Arts Council: 'If you don't increase the funding, we won't get the building.'

So you eventually took over a beautiful empty library around the corner from your original site. How did that come about?

Well, we were looking everywhere. There was a point at which we were sitting on short-term leases for around 25,000 square feet of disused office space around Shepherd's Bush. And we were allowing people to rehearse there – and that was quite a happy thing, to be able to support other small companies. But we got the agreement to use the old library building as a result of a mistake the council nearly made. There was this ancient deed of covenant with the Church of England, which said that unless that building was wholly used as a library or a museum, ownership of it would revert to the Church. And because the council had already moved their library to the newly built Westfield Centre, they were worried that the Church might reoccupy the old building. And I thought, if we can get in there, then psychologically, it will be harder to get us out later. So I called up Hammersmith council and said: 'Look, I've got an idea. While you resolve this thing with the Church of England, why don't we run a playtext library for you?' And they asked: 'How are you going to staff it?' So I said: 'Don't worry about it. I'll sort everything out. Just say yes.' So they said yes and I then phoned up all the publishers, Faber, Nick Hern and so on, and I said: 'Look, I need your whole back catalogue.' And brilliantly, they all sent their entire catalogue of playtexts.

So we built a little library space and opened the doors to the public during the day. We had playwrights sitting at what was left of the librarian's desk, and when members of the community wandered in off the street, they explained: 'It's a playtext library.' So you had people like James Graham and Nick Payne sitting with fingerless gloves on in the freezing cold, pretending to be librarians, while they wrote their plays.

I staffed it a couple of times, and I remember somebody walking in and asking: 'What is this?' I said: 'It's the Bush Theatre playtext library.' And they asked: 'What's the Bush Theatre?' They lived locally and they'd never heard of the Bush. It was an amazing moment for me – to see the benefit of having space that was publicly accessible in the daytime because suddenly, people could discover you were there when beforehand they had no idea.

Absolutely. And we ran this sort of publicity campaign. We got a company to give us these big billboards over the Westway and we put up a big picture of the library building with 'Bush Theatre' on the outside and a tagline which said: 'You don't know it yet, but I'm yours'. I think there's something very interesting and as yet unresolved really in what a publicly funded arts building is in this country. I've been really passionate about this at the Donmar. I think it should be a part of our education system to say: 'These theatres, these museums, these galleries, these libraries, these publicly funded things belong to you. They are part of the common good, and will, when you enter your working life, come from your taxes. And they are held in trust by us for you.'

One thing that has been a throughline of your work at both the Bush and the Donmar is your capacity to conceive of massive schemes. At the Bush we worked together on *Sixty Six Books* where we commissioned sixty-six writers to respond to the sixty-six books of the King James Bible. At the Donmar you did *The Vote*, which was broadcast live on TV on the night of the 2015 General Election. How do you go about conceiving these projects?

It's just the way my brain works, really – I think quite structurally. And for me there's always been an intimate relationship between how you use your different resources. That resource can be space or it can be people or it can be cash, and you have to think creatively about what you are doing with all of those. One of the great privileges of being an artistic director is that you're able to look at the entire shape of the organization and its budget and then define what you want to do in a radical and experimental form.

Something else I've done through pretty much my entire career as an artistic director is to commit to producing plays before they're finished. James Graham hadn't written anything when we announced *The Vote*. When the lighting grid fell out of the ceiling at the Bush, we announced a Broken Space season before anyone had written a word of any of those plays. I've got a great belief in empowering artists by just saying: 'We're doing it.'

That cuts against the conventional idea of how you produce a play, which says you should protect it until it's ready and then put it out into the world. That must be quite frightening at times?
Yes. It is about fear, but it is also about trust. I think it's our responsibility to interrogate what the impediments are to things happening. Some of them are reasonable impediments and some of them are historic impediments and some of them are daft impediments. One thing that I really wanted to do at the Donmar was to try, in really simple ways, to remove some of the impediments between artists and their work.

What does the notion of community mean to you? You've run two very different buildings in very different parts of London. How do you see each of those theatres' relationships with their local community, and what do you see is your responsibility in that regard?
It's complicated. At the Bush, when we got that amazing building in the heart of its community, what immediately happened is that people started saying: 'You know what, you should do children's theatre.' I got myself in a lot of trouble by saying that we were not going to do that. We would find ways to open the theatre up and make it accessible, but we needed to be really careful that its situation within its community didn't mean that we lost its mission, which was to produce the first and early plays of emerging writers.

But that mission doesn't have to be in conflict with being at the heart of a community. We certainly did work that was about the community.

For example, we commissioned a play about free schools, when Toby Young was opening the first free school around the corner. So things like that were good points for coming together. But I think the Bush needs to be for the whole of London and the whole of the country, in fact.

In terms of the Donmar, our education programme is disproportionate to the size of the theatre. And what's really important about that is that it goes out across all of the London boroughs. One of our targets is to try and make sure we are working with a school from every borough, not just the ones that are nearest to us, and we prioritize schools that have the highest proportion of free school meals.

The other really important challenge I faced when I took over was the fact that there was a perception that it was inaccessible to audiences. So we did a phenomenal amount of work to try and make tickets available in lots of different ways – particularly with cheap tickets through the Barclay's Front Row scheme and now with free tickets. And the audience has changed a lot. Not enough in my view, but they have changed a lot.

You spoke earlier on about being the first woman to run a major theatre in London. How do you see your role in relation to the wider issue of diversity in the industry?

I think probably our greatest achievement has been to have real diversity in the actors on our stage. Though that's relatively easy when you only do six shows a year and you're in the office sitting next to your casting director, you can absolutely set targets and make sure that it happens. For instance, *The Vote* was cast to the exact census data for Lambeth, where it was set. We had to go and find a Portuguese actor because there's a big Portuguese community there. So that was amazing and a really fascinating thing to see onstage. And the all-female Shakespeare trilogy was exactly about diversity of voice, class and background. Also, the percentage of women in our creative teams and women directors has also increased and that's been enormously important. We have set internal quotas – though we've not made a noise about that publicly. But we've absolutely ensured a 50/50 gender split.

And we have a significantly diverse workforce, but I don't think that we have enough diversity in our leadership. Yet, it's been amazing to have Kwame Kwei-Armah here as an associate – he's been a great voice within all that. I don't know if our audience is anything close to diverse enough. We keep going with that and we persist with it.

It's interesting with this film I am currently making about Mary Queen of Scots. That is a period drama where, historically, the characters would have all been white. But we have been fighting against that, and so, for instance, Adrian Lester is playing the English ambassador to the Scottish Court. And I felt massively empowered by the arguments we have been having in the theatre to make the case for that in a room full of film people.

Finally, who are the artistic directors whom you have found inspiring or who have mentored you?

In terms of their programming, Oskar Eustis at the Public is thrilling and inspiring. And I'm really enjoying what Rufus is doing at the National. I also think what Rupert Goold is doing at the Almeida is fabulous – I'm just always so thrilled to go see that work. And I loved the Royal Court under Dominic. I thought it was amazing – an incredible time for playwriting. Vicky Featherstone has minted that building's identity afresh and it is always a joy to see other women, such as her and Indhu Rubasingham running buildings.

In terms of mentors, Sam Mendes and Michael Grandage are both important because I trained under them. And Dominic Cooke has always been absolutely amazing; he's kind of my 'phone a friend' when I have a problem. Nick Hytner has also been significant to an extent – he's incredibly tough but in a brilliant way. He will ask the difficult questions and that's been really important.

15
INDHU RUBASINGHAM

Indhu Rubasingham became artistic director of the Tricycle Theatre in 2012. Situated in Brent, the most diverse borough in London, the venue has a seating capacity of 235 and has an international vision that aims to bring unheard voices into the mainstream. In April 2018 (after this interview was conducted) it was announced that the venue would be rebranded as Kiln Theatre to coincide with its reopening after an extensive capital redevelopment project.

Can you tell me about your journey to becoming artistic director of the Tricycle?

I discovered directing while I was studying drama at Hull University. When I graduated, I moved down to London and very fortunately got an Arts Council trainee director bursary to be an assistant director at Theatre Royal Stratford East under Jeff Teare and Philip Hedley. For the first time, I was able to see a building operate up close and receive a wide range of experience working on different shows: from the pantomime, to new writing, to musicals, to assisting Mike Leigh. Subsequently, I went on to a freelance career, predominantly directing new writing at places like the Royal Court, Hampstead Theatre, Chichester Festival Theatre, Birmingham Rep, Tricycle Theatre and the Liverpool Everyman as well as Theatre Royal Stratford East. At that point I'd always felt that being an artistic director would compromise your quality as an artist because you had to focus on doing too many different things at once. There were a few people I'd really respected as freelance directors whose work I felt was compromised when they took over a building.

I hadn't seriously thought about being an AD until the Tricycle job came up. I felt a lot of pressure to apply because I had such a strong relationship with the theatre. I remember at the time, I was directing at the Royal Court, and Dominic Cooke, the AD then, dragged me into his office and said: 'You are going to apply for this!' I was in such a dilemma about whether to apply or not – to the point where I had a real headache. I had no idea whether running a building was the right path for me.

Around this time my father passed away, and I think when you go through something like that, it shifts your landscape. So I thought: 'I'll apply and see what happens', and I found myself loving the application process because I just wrote down what I passionately believed in about the Tricycle and what I wanted it to be, rather than trying to impress the board. And, because I enjoyed that process, I thought: 'Even if I don't get the job this is a lovely way to help me understand my own freelance body of work, find the threads and pull them together into a bigger vision, and discover my own trajectory.' It's something I now tell younger directors to do, regardless of whether they are going for a job: 'Write down what you have been doing and your own personal mission statement', because it helps you articulate what drives you.

A couple of years into my time at the Gate, I re-read my own application and I thought: 'God, I actually did quite a lot of that. That's great!'

I know – it's nice to feel that it wasn't bullshit! It wasn't just saying things to try and get the job. What I'm really proud of is that a lot of the things I said I'd do, I've actually done – shows like *Red Velvet*, working with Sundance and so on. I remember getting the call to say that I'd got the job as the house lights were going down on a show I was about to watch. I felt utterly sick, as I realized it was too late to change my mind. But I then had this wonderful moment of realization. There was this artist whom I'd been working with for a while and we'd been trying to get his work on, and suddenly I thought: 'Oh, I can just do it – I don't have to convince someone else anymore!'

You mentioned that you'd felt that becoming an AD has compromised the quality of some other people's work. How do you think it affected your own work as a director?

I think I've always been a rigorous theatre director, but in some ways I think it has made me even more so since I have such pressure on my time now. I'll have a meeting before rehearsals, and again during my tea break, and then I'll have to finish early – so rehearsal time becomes very concentrated. I've become more focused and I think that's brought a sharpness but, at the same time, there's a lack of ability to sometimes give things air or to be a bit more open; so I think that the gain in one respect is a loss in another.

When you took over at the Tricycle, your predecessor, Nick Kent, had been running it for a very long time indeed and it had a very clear identity with all of the verbatim work and the clear political focus.

Yes. He had been there twenty-eight years and had done it brilliantly, making it a huge success.

How did you find the process of taking over?

I think there's a whole book I could write about this! In business circles they talk about change management, and though the Tricycle is a small organization, it struggled with that. Everyone appeared to be up for change, but change involves challenging whole structures and systems – things that are really entrenched – so you had to ask: 'Are they really up for it?' Because no matter what people say, 95 per cent of human nature is resistant to change. It's scary, unknown and unsafe. It was insane to go into running a building, instigating a big change in culture and structure, without ever having run a building before.

It's a fascinating and quite lovely thing about our theatre culture that boards are often very happy to gift somebody a big organization, purely on the basis of their artistry. That seems both absolutely crazy and kind of liberating at the same time.

Yes. But I would stand by that. If we begin to think that artists haven't got the knowledge to be a chief executive, or need to have their hand held by a consultant, then that can be really dangerous. Organizations need to be artistically led with very strong support and I will fight tooth and nail until I retire or die for that. When I started, I remember someone suggested that maybe I shouldn't be chief executive, so that I could concentrate on the work on stage, but I said no because what I believe in has to be imbued throughout the building from the moment that someone walks in. A vision is more than the work on stage; it's about the ethos and culture of the whole organization and the values it carries.

Otherwise, I could be doing a certain kind of work on stage, while someone else decides to turn the bar and the cafe into a fine dining restaurant. And how would that fit with the vision? Theatres have to be risk taking, they have to think outside the box, they have to bring in new audiences and be relevant. Therefore, the leadership has to come from an artistic instinct, in my opinion.

One thing that I think is really interesting when you take over an organization is how you learn that some of the things that people internally think are facts turned out to be myths. For instance, the Tricycle never used to have allocated seating. When I started, everyone was adamant you couldn't get allocated seating without changing the theatre, but a year later, after a number of sold-out shows and audiences complaining, we found a way to get allocated seating in there. It was an absolute myth that it wasn't possible.

So I would absolutely support any new artistic director coming into a building to find their own voice and stamp their own ground. Be your own person. You got the job because they wanted you to do the job. Sure, you will make mistakes, but we're not hospitals; hopefully we're not going to end up killing people. We're artists and we have to thrive on change and mistakes. Nick Kent made the Tricycle into an incredible political powerhouse, and I'm absolutely honouring that journey but doing it in a different way.

One thing I ask myself now, given that I seem to have done all right at the job, is: 'Why did I not go into this earlier? What stopped me?' And because I'm politically minded, I've always been interested in more than just directing what's on the stage, so I find that I'm annoyed with myself because I've realized how one can convince oneself of things which aren't necessarily true. Another myth. I look back on it now, and I realize the problem was that I didn't believe that I could be an artistic director because I never saw anyone like me doing it when I started out. They were predominately white men, and the majority were from Oxbridge. I think I subconsciously held an inner belief that 'that world is not for me'. But I was never going to articulate that to myself. I deluded myself into believing that that world wasn't for me because it would compromise my artistic drive. As a result, I'm interested in not only the external barriers that prevent us but also the internal barriers that may stop us from aspiring to certain things.

It feels, at the moment, like that white male, Oxbridge grip on the theatre might be loosening a little. We have people of colour appointed to some really major venues in recent years such as National Theatre of Wales, the Bush, Theatre Royal Stratford East and the Young Vic. So maybe change is happening?
Yes. And you do need the white male Oxbridge directors, but there needs to be an equal playing field. There needs to be an equality of opportunity for those different voices. The diversity of leadership in terms of class, race, gender, age and ability will ensure a thriving range of taste and opinions and perspectives.

How do you go about putting a season together?
It's a curious process – long in the planning, chaos in the delivery! It's about honouring our mission, taking risks and balancing the books. The programme, up until we closed for our capital project, was made up of a mixture of received work, co-productions and in-house Tricycle productions, which cost more to produce. So the challenge is: 'How do you find a clever way to curate a season, so it comes under the same umbrella of the mission statement?' What's great about the Tricycle is that we're not bent on making one type of work, though I do have a natural interest in new writing. I think that if you want to amplify diverse voices and create different lenses through which to view the world, then you're more likely to get that in new writing.

Of course, it is important to find plays that will attract and entertain audiences. The plays I look for need to feel substantial and amplify big ideas to fill the Tricycle. Alongside this, we also have to take risks and challenge perspectives.

To take one specific season as an example: in 2013, I brought an American actor, Colman Domingo, over to do his one-man show called *A Boy and His Soul*. I knew that it wouldn't necessarily be a big seller initially because he was unknown, but it could be a slow-burn once the word got out. I then did a new play *Handbagged* by Moira Buffini, which was my mid-risk because I didn't know how a new play would be received. And the show I was most confident about when programming was *Once a Catholic* by Mary O'Malley and directed by Kathy Burke, which was a known text and would appeal to our local community. We also brought *Red Velvet* back, which I knew would sell out because of the success of the original run. The risk in doing *Handbagged* paid off because it hugely appealed to the audiences and then went on to have further life in the West End and touring nationally. That was a successful season!

It often feels to me, when programming, that you have to find a balance between supporting the ambitions of the artists you are interested in and supporting the appetite of the audience. The ideal thing is when you can make the two match. But if you try too hard to just give the audience what they want, it can end up feeling quite hollow, and if you focus too much on the artist's vision to the exclusion of all else, you can end up with no one wanting to see the show.

I think there's another danger in between those two extremes. I've had shows, like *Red Velvet* and *Handbagged*, whose success surprised me because they were initially just plays that I really believed in. However, when you're seen as someone who can pick plays that attract audiences, you can start to second-guess your choices. You question whether you're interested in a project because you anticipate it will transfer into the West End when, actually, transferring shows cannot be the sole measure of a successful production. Doing something bold that appeals to your local audience, to your Tricycle audience, is still a success. If we are focused on finding the next hit then we may find that we're not taking the right risks on emerging writers, directors and actors, and this is something I have to keep in check. You have to hold on to your gut instincts and make sure you don't become too canny or too calculating.

One word we use a lot in the industry is 'community'. What does that mean to you in relation to the Tricycle?

It is a word that gets used a lot and there are different communities. With the Tricycle, there's obviously the local community, but within that local community, there are several hundred cultural communities as well as different age groups. There's also the artistic/industry community, which I feel very proud of and is a privilege to be part of.

My big thing at the Tricycle is to ask: 'How do you get those people in who are alienated by theatre and who don't think it's for them?' I come very much from that ethos. I had really supportive parents, but they didn't believe theatre was for them. If it wasn't for my own experience at school, I wouldn't be here. I have this memory from when I started as AD at the Tricycle, of watching a middle-aged Middle Eastern man and this young kid, probably his son, walk halfway up the corridor of the Tricycle and then turn around and walk out. My narrative for them was that the narrow corridor into the building became too intimidating for them to continue on that journey. Those are the people I'm really curious about.

Equally, when people talk about theatre for communities, they often think that it means making work for the lowest common denominator. I'm not interested in that at all. I want the Tricycle's work to be of a very high quality, but I also want the audiences to be from as many different local communities as possible. I want them to feel comfortable in the space with whoever they are rubbing shoulders with. We definitely get a very diverse audience – culturally, gender and age-wise – and sometimes we'll have a show that really lands beautifully for all of them. It's bringing those groups together which matters.

It can be quite a challenge to create a space that works for those wealthy individuals upon whose support the theatre relies while still making it accessible for a much wider group of people. You might be making work for which the primary audience is not actually the people who paid for it.

Yes, but this was the case for a long time, even before Shakespeare. I also don't think, if you're a donor, that you're going to engage with the Tricycle in Kilburn without somehow understanding the nature of the work or the politics of it. That said, when I started the job I had a real fear about my lack of experience in fundraising. I thought: 'I've never done it. I'm not well connected enough.'

I think if people are interested in your work, then you're halfway there. If you're the kind of supporter who merely wants a good time, to have a nice dinner and to be meeting the right kind of people, then you're not likely to want to support the Tricycle, whereas if you're invested in the Tricycle's work, and in the politics and in the area, then you will want to support. And I now have a confidence to say: 'This is where I'm going. You can come with me on this journey, but if you don't like it, please don't feel you have to.' You have to bring the right people with you, so you maintain your vision and integrity.

We are currently living through a very particular political moment – with Brexit and Trump and so on. What role do you think theatre has to play within that wider situation?
First, we should be careful not to over emphasize our importance because sometimes we do like to think we can heal the world! However, what theatre and the arts can do is provide a safe space for nuanced debate and enable people to walk in someone else's shoes. As artists, we like complexity and believe in the tenet that there are many truths: there's your truth, there's my truth and there's a bigger truth. And what we can do is create a safe space for contrary ideas to be expressed and explored. I think there's a danger – when all this shit is going on – of jumping on to bandwagons or resorting to quick slogans or of being judgemental in our thinking and leaving no space for grey areas. And that's where theatre can be really important and it is what theatre and artists thrive on.

Also, theatre is a space for gathering people, and it may be that they are like-minded people, in a way that a church gathers like-minded people. And that's not necessarily a bad thing. The worst thing that can happen is that, as cultural leaders, we become scared. There is a risk that we won't want to cause controversy because we're afraid of our funding being cut or we're afraid of creating enemies. So we have to be battle-ready.

Who are the artistic directors who have inspired or excited you?
Oh, there are so many. I loved Neil Bartlett for his work even before he ran the Lyric in Hammersmith – when he was running his own company: Gloria; David Lan at the Young Vic; Dominic Cooke at the Royal Court; Ruth Mackenzie when she was at Nottingham Playhouse; Daniel Evans when he was at Sheffield; and Rufus Norris at the National. And, of course, I started under Stephen Daldry at the Royal Court, which was a very exciting time. And Nick Hytner is a great mentor to me. When I started the job, he told me: 'Do what you really believe in and then see how it goes.' And I have always tried to stick to that.

16
HOWARD SHALWITZ

Howard Shalwitz ran the Woolly Mammoth Theatre Company from 1978 until 2018 as its founding artistic director. Woolly Mammoth is based in Washington, DC, and primarily produces new plays in its 265-seat auditorium.

Could you tell me about your journey to becoming artistic director at Woolly Mammoth Theatre?

I did a lot of theatre in high school but I come from a family of doctors, so at college I was a pre-med and then a philosophy major. Then I did a master's degree in teaching, heading towards a career as a high school social studies teacher. I was very interested in educational philosophy and policy. But just at the point where I would have accepted a teaching job I said: 'I'm not going to do that. Let me take a year off and do some acting.' That was in 1976 and I'm still taking my year off!

So I went off to New York to do the acting thing. And I became friends with Roger Brady, a fellow intern at the New Jersey Shakespeare Festival, and we began talking about starting a theatre company together. This went on for about three or four years. Finally, we did a couple of shows under the name Woolly Mammoth as far off-Broadway as you can imagine in New York. As we got serious about it, we explored different cities around the country and we ended up picking Washington, I think, partly because it was the nation's capital. We had an interest in political and topical work, as well as in aesthetic exploration and provocation.

We started here literally knocking on doors of churches and schools and all sorts of public buildings to see if we could find a place to perform. We held our first auditions outdoors in a public park. We had no money to get the theatre started, but our first venue was an Episcopal church downtown. (To this day I have a love of Episcopalians because they were so good to us!) It was a downtown church that had several arts groups in residence. Because a lot of their local population had moved away, they were using the arts as part of the broader framework for attracting people to a parish where no one lived in anymore. They gave us a home for five or six years, and that's where we sort of established ourselves. And then we were in another space for thirteen years, and there were some nomadic periods, but finally we landed in this incredible space we're in now, on our twenty-fifth anniversary.

Why are you called Woolly Mammoth?

Well, we were drunk! One night, the co-founder of the theatre, Roger Brady, and I were just drunk and we were cooking up names for the theatre. We have, in our archives, a list of about a hundred names we made that night, and Woolly Mammoth is on there. And it's actually spelled right too. It's the British spelling because there's an American spelling of the word 'woolly', which is W-O-O-L-Y. That is an arcane fact of dictionary history!

It's fascinating that your first home was in an Episcopalian church. I'm interested in how theatres are sort of secular churches, and I feel like artistic directors almost have the role of a kind of secular minister, don't they?

I think that is especially the case if you're a founder, as I am. But I think any artistic director is not really in the business of putting plays on and selling tickets. It looks that way, but I've always said that running a theatre is much more like running a church than a restaurant. You're in the business of constantly converting people to a way of behaving together and a way of seeing the world. And I think especially with a company like Woolly, which is always trying to push the envelope, we can count on the fact that people won't like every show they see in a year.

It's probably harder for us to sell subscriptions, which is the American model, compared to theatres that put out seasons that combine classics and last year's New York and London hits. At Woolly, for the most part, no one's heard of any of the plays we're going to do in any given season. Generally, we're trying to convince people of our taste, of the adventure that Woolly represents, of our way of enquiring into new ways of thinking about theatre and into the impact that we believe theatre can have on the world. So we're converting them to a sort of ideology if you will, rather than thinking: 'Oh, we're selling products.'

How has being in Washington shaped you and the mission of the company?

Washington has changed hugely, especially in its cultural scene, since we first came here. So, just in terms of the theatre scene, when we moved here the main place was Arena Stage which had been founded a couple of decades earlier and was one of the famous flagships of the American regional theatre movement.

But Woolly was part of a wave of 'alternative theatres' which sprang up in the late 1970s and early 1980s – in the decade after the off-Broadway movement in New York. We associated with protest theatre, anti-Vietnam work, and a lot of adventurous writers like Sam Shepard. We were dubbed 'alternatives' in the beginning, and I wear that proudly because I think we saw ourselves as an alternative to what the mainstream regional theatres were doing: we were trying to do newer work, and more adventurous and provocative work.

So how do you start the programming process? Do you always start with the writer? How do you pick the plays and the artists, and then how do you shape that season?

It's evolved a lot. Our very early seasons, when we were just starting out, were a mix of European avant-garde classics: plays by Mrożek or Pinter, or Boris Vian, though we did also do some of the newer, more aggressive, young American writers of the time – people like Mark Medoff and Jean-Claude Van Itallie. But after four or five seasons, we decided to focus mainly on American work with the occasional British or Canadian play in there too. Then, after about ten years, we narrowed that focus to be mostly on new American plays, where we were working with the writer. Then, moving into the 1990s, our work began heading in much more diverse directions – we were really trying to include more women and more writers of colour. The goal was always to avoid the comfortable middle. So it's not like we had any particular house style, but we didn't do the comfortable kitchen sink dramas that still predominate in American writing.

I think the political angle of our work really took off when we moved into this new space. Some people describe Woolly as a theatre that was always critiquing the American Dream. I'm not sure that that's quite accurate, but I'll accept that our work often critiques notions of American exceptionalism and so on. But when we moved into this venue, which was so much bigger than where we'd been before, I really felt that family scale plays – you know with father/son or mother/daughter relationship issues- were just not big enough for the scale of the venue and the location. We're a stone's throw from the National Archives. You can walk just a block away and see the Capitol at one end and the Washington Monument at the other. So we felt that if you came to our theatre, it had to give you something of substance to talk about.

In about 2009/2010 we developed a community engagement strategy called Connectivity where we explicitly started looking at each play as a platform for a community conversation. So now we really look at every script and ask: 'Is there a significant conversation here that would engage our community and our audience in something of importance?' And if not, even if I like the play, even if I find it experimental as a piece of writing, I'm not likely to do it.

The ideal Woolly play should combine both civic and aesthetic provocation. I've always felt that when writers have new and provocative things to say, they usually find new and provocative ways to say it. I think that if a play tries to spoon-feed the audience in too comfortable a way, it won't actually engage them in the conversation. When you're asking an audience to engage in the style, format, structure or language of a play in some fresh way, you can lead them into the civic and political dialogue that the play contains. Of course, some writers would completely disagree with me and say that if you complicate things aesthetically, you don't get to the direct civic engagement, but these are all matters of opinion.

How would you define the community that Woolly Mammoth serves? And how do you see your own role in relation to that collection of people?

I think we've all come to loathe the word 'community' because it's been so overused for about twenty years without necessarily being defined very clearly. But I think there has been a huge change over the thirty-seven to thirty-eight years of Woolly's history. During our foundational period, the audiences were mostly white. But I do think we've always attracted both older and younger audiences. And I've always felt that young audiences and old audiences both bring something great to the theatre. In Washington, in particular, I think audiences across the whole age spectrum can be very adventurous.

So most theatres, certainly in a diverse city like Washington, are programming for many, many different audiences. The 64,000-dollar question today is: How do we get those audiences to come together? How do we not programme in a kind of tokenistic way where you have your 'black slot' and your 'gay slot' and your 'Latino slot' and so on? That's a question that we're very much engaged in at Woolly right now. We're asking ourselves fundamental questions like: 'What is the sort of psychographic profile that cuts across all of our audiences?' And we think that they have a certain thirst for adventure. So we're asking: 'How do we turn that into a values proposition?' If someone came here for the first time because we did some community outreach or because they had a personal affinity with the topic of a particular play or because we gave them a free ticket, or whatever, how do we then say to them: 'Why don't you come back to witness and be part of the conversation we're having with other communities?' Statistically, about a quarter of our audience identify themselves as people of colour, right now. But we feel that's not good enough, and we need to go much further.

As a DC-based theatre, how do you see your relationship with New York?

We have great relationships with a lot of theatres in New York, and we collaborate with them. For instance, Playwrights Horizons commissioned *Dead Man's Cell Phone* by Sarah Ruhl. But they let us premiere it, and then they did it later.

Why would they do that?

Because New York theatres recognize that there is a danger zone for plays that premiere in New York. If they get a bad review from the *New York Times*, that can be the kiss-of-death for the whole future of the play. So in a way, by sometimes having a play premiere out of town, it gives the writer a little more cushioning from the New York scene. Another example is Anne Washburn's *Mr Burns*. That was commissioned by The Civilians – a devising ensemble in New York – but they approached us to actually premiere it. Maybe they thought we could marshal more resources for it while it was still developing. And it just kind of clicked with our sensibility and we gave it what I thought was a brilliant premiere here at Woolly. But actually, even before we premiered it, we had developmental support from Seattle Rep, another big regional theatre, and from Playwrights Horizons in New York: there was a workshop at both of those theatres. So there is a lot of healthy working together, and I think that that's a really important development in the field over the last fifteen years.

A key thing for us is that we are not possessive about new plays. Bruce Norris's *Clybourne Park* is another good example. We were the first theatre to commit to it – we had it in our season and were going to premiere it. But then Bruce said: 'Playwrights Horizons wants to do it, but they have a slot a little bit earlier than you.' And we said: 'Of course'. Now, sure, in hindsight it won the Pulitzer Prize, so it would have been great to have had the premiere credit. But really that doesn't matter to us that much.

One area where there is a difference is that we're not a playwrights' theatre in the same way that, for example, Playwrights Horizons is. So there are certain cultural norms about how New York theatres work which don't apply to us. Woolly has a company of artists, including one playwright, Robert O'Hara; several directors who are among the best in the country; fifteen to twenty actors; and a group of designers. So tension can arise where a playwright might say: 'I want to premiere a play at a theatre where I can pick any actor, from any city, and cast everybody from New York.' But that's not what Woolly does.

I've always believed that an ensemble spirit, where artists have worked together over time, just leads to better work. An ideal Woolly production usually has about a third to a half of artists who are company members or other Woolly veterans, and then maybe a third to a half are people we're working with us for the first time. And I've seen the power of that balance over many years.

Another thing that differentiates us is that through our Connectivity strategy, we will often say to a writer: 'Well, who's the ideal audience you want for your play?' A lot of times we find that writers have never even heard that question before. They've never asked themselves: 'What audience do I want?' So they just say: 'I don't know, whoever comes into your theatre.' But we like to think a little more strategically about why we're picking plays and what our purpose is in terms of the conversation we're trying to start with the play and who, in our community in the nation's capital, we want to get into the theatre.

So these are examples of how there is no 'one size fits all' in terms of how the American theatre works. At Woolly we often find ourselves having to say to writers: 'Well, you might expect a certain kind of experience at other theatres, either in New York or in the bigger regional venues where they have more resources than we do; but here's how we can bring value to your play in a different way.'

What role do you take in the development of each show? If you are not directing the show yourself, how do you manage your relationship with the writer, director and creative team?

I have a really talented literary director, and at different points, I've had associate artistic directors, and it is usually they who are on the front lines in terms of engaging with the writer on a regular basis. What I try to do is to stay far enough away from the project so that I can then 'swoop in' once in a while and give reasonably objective feedback. I always try to be very forthright and very direct. But I never make the assumption that anyone has to take my point of view. I just have to be as persuasive as I can. I'll probably give notes about half a dozen times, throughout the life of a project – at various different stages: first day of rehearsals, the designer run-through, dress rehearsal, a couple of previews and so on.

The unique thing about being an artistic director, at least in my experience, is that you are able to position yourself as an audience member a little more easily than you can when you're the director or writer of a project. What an artistic director does, for better or worse, is to internalize the flavour, the voice and the mindset of the audience that comes to the theatre. That's a key part of the job: to be in that unique nexus between the art making and the audience making.

But overall, our job is to take risks. And if you take risks it means that some of them aren't going to pay off, but you still want them to, every time. Something you learn over time is that the line between success and failure is razor thin. I can think of one project, which I won't name, that was one of the most successful plays we've ever done and which has now been produced all over the world. But after a workshop that we did six months before rehearsal started, I was ready to pull the plug. My associate artistic director had to talk me down from the ledge because I just thought: 'Oh my God, nobody's going to get this. They're not going to like it. They're going to think that it's terrible.' So then you have to step back from that and go: 'We're committed to this project. How can we add value to it? What are the steps that we can take to move it forward to the finish line?'

Back in the late 1990s there was a lot of talk in the American new writing world, about how theatres were workshopping plays to death. There were articles in the *New York Times* about how writers could get readings and workshops but they couldn't get productions. At the time, Woolly had its own reading series. We'd do four or five staged readings a year where we'd spend a day working with the writer and throw something up for an audience to respond to. At that point I said: 'Well, let's not be part of the problem. Let's be part of the solution. Let's stop doing what I call 'speculative development' and let's put all of our energy into identifying projects we believe in and that we want to take a risk on, and developing them because we're actually going to do them.' And that's really been our philosophy ever since. We really don't do commissions of projects where we're going to only produce one out of three. So I'm definitely an artistic director who really does trust my own judgement of a play on the printed page. I've learned also, over too many years of doing staged readings and stuff like that, that those can be as deceptive as anything else. So generally I like the philosophy of basically putting all our eggs into the basket of the plays we're actually producing. I've learnt to trust my own judgement and the judgement of my staff, and just say: 'This is a play we believe in. Let's do it.'

Finally, who are the artistic directors who have really inspired you?

Two people come to mind. One is someone who died recently and that's Zelda Fichandler, the founder of Arena Stage. I became good friends with Zelda in the last five or six years of her life because she moved back to Washington after she finished her work at NYU. And so we would get together once in a while, and she became a big fan of Woolly Mammoth. It's interesting because in the early days of Woolly, I looked at Arena Stage, the flagship regional theatre, and said: 'That's everything we don't want to be. We are an alternative to that. They're doing the easy stuff. We're doing the hard, new, edgy stuff.'

But when I really got to know Zelda, I realized that she had the same revolutionary zeal when she started Arena, that I had when I started

Woolly, and the two of us talked about it all the time. She too wanted to change the landscape of theatre, which in her case was about a field that was all concentrated in New York. The idea of making work in a regional setting, with a company of artists and more of a European model, was a really revolutionary idea. And then, on top of that, they combined both classics and some powerful new work. It's just that by the time I was coming up, those seemed like old plays to me, but they weren't when she was first doing them. I always say to young people, going into the theatre: 'There really isn't a field for you to learn how to plug yourself into. Sure, you need some skills, but really if you're entering the field of theatre, especially as a director, or a playwright, your job is to remake it, and I think that's what everyone's job is.' So that's one of the things that I really took from my relationship with Zelda, and she was incredibly inspiring and very encouraging to me.

More recently, though, what Blanka Zizka is doing at the Wilma Theatre in Philadelphia, is very exciting to me. She came here as a refugee from Czechoslovakia, in the late 1970s and started the Wilma Theatre which has now moved into a beautiful mid-sized venue in downtown Philadelphia. In the last five or six years I have got increasingly frustrated with what I call 'the assembly line' model of producing theatre. This is where you have too short a rehearsal process and you start with the playwright, and then the director comes on board, and then the designers do their work, and then the actors don't show up until a few weeks before the thing goes into tech. It's just not an organic process in the way that you might get in a European company, where you could touch base with that project and with the artists who are going to do it, over a long period of time.

But Blanka took a very aggressive approach to solving that problem for herself. She raised a lot of money and invited European directors and theatre trainers to work with that company and build up their skills. She has also invited major international directors to direct productions: Theodoros Terzopoulos, from Greece, did a brilliant *Antigone* there and Csaba Horvath from Hungary did *Blood Wedding*. In a funny way, I feel like she's saying that the American field is on some level broken so long as we continue to stick to the basic way that we normally work, and that we have to find ways to get outside of that. So she's putting her money where her mouth is and trying to figure out how to do that in a really novel way.

17
NIEGEL SMITH

Niegel Smith has been artistic director of The Flea Theatre since 2015. An off-off-Broadway space, The Flea recently moved to new premises in Tribeca. It has three performance spaces all with fewer than ninety-nine seats. It exists to support early career artists and to: 'champion those voices least likely to be at the forefront of our culture'.

What was your journey to becoming artistic director of The Flea?
I always imagined that there would be a leadership component to my work. As a young professional, my original dreams were of serving specific communities through my art. I imagined a model much like the Cornerstone Theater in LA that Bill Rauch used to run and which is now run by Michael John Garcés. Cornerstone began by travelling around the country and making work with different communities before it eventually landed as an LA-based theatre company.

Augusto Boal and his Forum Theatre work have also influenced me. When I was an undergrad he came to do a residency with us. There were two things about his work that struck a chord with me: firstly, his idea of the 'cop and the head'. This is about making something dramatic out of the psychological trauma imposed by outside voices on one's existence – so it has a theatre therapy component to it. As a survivor of deep trauma, it was really compelling for me to explore how one's personal history can be opened up in a theatrical space – and how that can lead to action and character in a dramatic situation. Ultimately, I believe that our ability to tell and to imagine a story directly affects how we live our life. Secondly, I was influenced by the work he did through Forum Theatre – which involved directly engaging with the community to explore big questions through art.

Where were you studying?
At Dartmouth, up in rural New Hampshire. I was a double minority there – as a gay, black man. I felt a lot of outsiderness and that influenced the kinds of work that I was making and that I was pulled towards. So there I was, a young artist, thinking: 'I'm going to use this form that I'm working in to serve communities'. Then I got pulled to New York even though I never thought I would end up here.

Why?
Well, I grew up in rural North Carolina and then Detroit. And Detroit was a city in decline when I was there. We had a mayor, Coleman Young, who had been there for eighteen years at that point. And there was a lot of corruption in city government. Because of the riots in the late 1960s, there had been white flight and disinvestment in the city. Because of the crack epidemic, homes were not very safe spaces. The streets were not very safe spaces. There was a lot of trauma and death and destruction and a lack of care. So I thought, having come from a rural place: 'Oh, this is what a city is.' I thought: 'Cities are not places that nurture me or nourish me. Why would I ever want to live in one?'

That's interesting because one might think that as a gay, black man from somewhere rural, a city like New York would be an obvious place to be drawn to.
I know, one might think that, but no! Cities were hard at the beginning because there were so many people, so much death, so much destruction, so much roughness. I had severe anxiety at the time; even walking in public spaces with lots of people was hard. Sometimes I would have to step to the side and go into a doorway and just breathe for a little bit in order to then keep going.

But I got an opportunity to work with the then artistic director of the Public, George Wolfe, and with Tony Kushner and Jeanine Tesori on the musical *Caroline, Or Change*, and I wasn't going to pass that up! I then ended up assisting George in the producing office at the Public – which was a theatre that I felt lived out my values day to day. George has never taken on a theatrical project that he does not believe in fully and totally. And I'd made a decision very early on in my career that that's the only kind of work I would do – no matter what that meant financially.

I was assisting as much as I could on the curation of new work there: particularly though the New Works Now Initiative. This was 2004 and I'd successfully lobbied for this play that was about a trans boy. And George calls me over and says: 'I heard you like this play, so I'm gonna put it in the festival and you should direct it.' It was a great moment, and it taught me a great deal about leadership and about the importance of identifying people's passions. Because in my young artist's mind, I thought we would get an established artist to direct it. But the values of that institution are about supporting passion and desire, and giving people space to develop.

So I've always wanted to serve specific communities, to make work that looks like the world around me, and to champion voices that may not have space in the mainstream. Developing artists has always been just as important to me as being an interpreter of existing plays. The day I found out about the AD job at The Flea, I got three separate emails from colleagues saying: 'The Flea's looking for an artistic director. You should apply.' I'd seen a few things there and I'd had one of my best moments in the theatre when I went to see *The Vandals*. Before the show started, someone came up to do a speech and said: 'Hello. I'm a Bat, a member of the resident company here at The Flea Theatre.' And I thought: 'There's a resident company here in New York City? How come I didn't know this?' This was particularly interesting to me, given my huge love for community and for the development of artists.

So when I applied, it felt very right. This was partly because of its commitment to early career artists but also because it made work not for any kind of commercial sensibility but rather for the sake of the art itself. It's a space that is exuberant and exciting but also pushes you and makes you uncomfortable. Those are hallmarks of the kind of work I make and the kind of work that I most enjoy. So I knew I didn't need to come in and shake it up or rethink the mission. I could just become a steward of that mission.

What does the word 'community' mean to you? What communities does The Flea serve?

Part of my vision is for The Flea to be the hub at the centre of a wheel, with the spokes going out into the community. So either we might create things out in the community and then bring the people to the theatre. Or we might be at the theatre and then go out to the community. We're a community centre that puts rigorous, high-quality art at the heart of dialogue. We're there as a place for people to be both affirmed and challenged. We are not a museum, not a place to just go and see the things done beautifully.

In terms of specific groups, historically, a major part of our community has been early career artists. They make work here and they come to see their peers' work that speaks directly to their experience. Then there is a middle-aged and older community who is interested in work that asks tough political and social questions about the world around us. So there's a huge overlap with places like Soho Rep and The Public and the Culture Project that used to be on Bleeker Street.

In terms of communities that I'm hoping to develop, I think that we have an opportunity to reach out in our geographic community – places around us like Chinatown, Tribeca and Lower Manhattan. And this is where our all ages programming begins because there are lots of young people and their families out there. And we have work specifically about the Chinese experience under commission. So I'm hopeful that people in those geographic communities will begin to see The Flea as somewhere that is not just a place to go see good art, but which is making art that is reflective of and wrestling with their own experiences.

There is currently a big conversation around diversity in the theatre in both the UK and the United States. Am I right in thinking that you are one of the few people of colour who run a theatre in New York?

In New York City, I know of three other artistic directors of colour. One is Ty Jones at Classical Theatre of Harlem, and then there is Jonathan McCrory at National Black Theatre, and there is Shay Wafer at 651 Arts in Brooklyn. I think what is unique to me is that I'm the only African American artistic director of a theatre that is not culturally specific – though I hope that will change. I was talking with my agent the other day about how the only offers that I, and my African American peers, get are for black plays. When I direct plays that are not about the African or African American experience, it's because I've been a part of their development and already have a relationship with the playwright. But producers don't see me in that way.

So to be running a theatre that is not just focused through one very specific lens is unique. And that is problematic for the field because it means that the majority of work is actually being produced from the point of view of a single, predominantly white, culture. And this means that you end up with institutions that only produce work that, dramaturgically, has an Aristotelian worldview as its primary mode for storytelling. Luckily for me, I come from African and African American roots and so a circular worldview is part of what I bring to the artistic equation.

What is that circular worldview?
Many African countries and cultures actually see time as circular – so what you're experiencing has already been experienced. You're just returning back to it. And if you exist not on a line but on a circle, then that changes the structure of a theatrical event.

How might that worldview manifest itself in your programming?
Well, I'm about to direct a show called *Syncing Ink* that is a freestyle hip-hop play. It's the coming-of-age story of a young black boy growing up outside of Baltimore. What happens is that a group of òrìṣà – Yoruban gods – come to him and say: 'You're not fulfilling your part of the plan, the circle. The circle of the hip-hop cipher is broken because you are not leading with your voice. You haven't synced in with your oral tradition.' So instead of being a character that is beginning in one place and going to another place, he's actually just stepping into a broken circle and completing that circle. The whole thing is a hip-hop ritual. It's staged in the round and the audience is in the round, so we're in a communal situation.

Beyond programming, what do you see as the wider role that an artistic director has?
Being a champion is part of the role that I like the most – being a cheerleader for the form. I go sit on panels and I talk about the problems that are facing us or the successes we have had. I go to meetings or galas and I give speeches and get people excited about the transformative elements of the theatre. I report on how audience members or artists have been changed or helped or aided or fulfilled by their work. I go to our city leaders and request more funding or support for the arts. And I have a working knowledge, not just of what my theatre is doing for the ecology of the arts in our city but what other theatres are doing so I can say 'hoorah' for that too.

How do you go about working with other directors once you have employed them to make a show?
I love being with the director and the playwright throughout the process. I love being that person who gets to help them suss out what they're attempting to do. My job isn't to interpret the world or write the world of their play but rather to help them articulate it better. Navigating that relationship is extremely complex. As someone who directs for a living, I could easily become very prescriptive, saying: 'Change this. Make this. Do this.' So my job is just to help you get closer to the thing that you're trying to get to, and to reveal to you things that you might not realize.

I got some really great advice from Jack Reuler who runs Mixed Blood Theatre in Minneapolis, which is another theatre that lives out the values that I care about. He said: 'When you offer a director a job, you can put anything on the table. You can say, "You have to cast this actor. You have to use this designer. You have to do blah, blah, blah." But once you've hired them, you've hired them to make all the rest of those choices. You can advise them and you can champion certain choices. But when they make a choice, you have to support it fully. If you don't do that, then you end up undermining them.'

Yes. And you have to empower people to be able to disagree with you; otherwise they might just make whatever choice they think will please the boss.
That can especially be the case with early career playwrights. They tend to want to please you because they want you to do their work and they think you know what will be successful. But we say to playwrights: 'Look, you have to know what play you want to write. We hired you because of your voice and the play that you're on the trajectory of writing.' And I might say to them: 'Maybe, if I was sitting in your chair, I'd try this or that,' but ultimately, they've got to be willing to say: 'No, that's not the play.'

We talk about 'taking risks' a lot in theatre. What does that mean to you?
I think it means engaging with questions that I don't know the answer to. Every season there needs to be a couple plays where I have no idea how they will come into fruition. This will be where there is something pulsating about a play that grabs me: maybe in its language, or its

worldview or its dramaturgy. And I will think: 'That thing is brilliant and we need to wrestle with it. The audience need to wrestle with it.' But there will still be a ton of questions around it. That, to me, is primarily what a risk is.

Another important area for risk is with the early career directors who become our resident directors. They may have few professional credits to their name when they begin at The Flea, but when I accept them as a resident director, they are guaranteed to get productions. And that's a huge risk. But over the course of their time with us, I develop a relationship with them as an artist, so there's a great amount of mentorship that goes on. One other way we take risks is when we turn over the theatre to our resident company, the Bats, for their shows. We are taking a risk because we are willing to give over the keys to the castle.

The Bats are a brilliant company, but obviously they all work voluntarily. So how do you ensure that your institutional relationship with them is genuinely supportive rather than exploitative?

We are an off-off-Broadway theatre and so the scale that we're making stuff on is not a scale that supports making a living out of the art. But I think about this a lot in terms of my early career. When I graduated college, I wanted to make my first professional show and I didn't have any wealth. I was an intern making $75 a week. So I held auditions for volunteer actors to be part of the production that I was putting together. I found a sound designer who worked in a dress shop where the owner said: 'Nothing's happening here after 6 pm. Do something with the space then.' And my grandmother got her pastor to have a special collection at church one Sunday and then sent me $600, which I used to cover the props and costumes and give the actors a little money. But essentially, we were a group of people, who somehow had to make the show even though we didn't have resources.

So The Flea serves a specific function in the ecology of New York. Young artists come to the city and want to make work, but they don't yet have or they've never had financial support to make their art. And neither do they have professional relationships to call on or the credits to go work in an equity show. So The Flea supports them by taking on the work of fundraising and managing things so that they have the space to be creative. Because it is voluntary, people can say: 'This is not right for me right now' and move away. Every role has a backup so that if something happens during the course of a show, like you get a paid gig, then you can go do that paid gig. The shows are not about using you up. They're about serving you. But it's a tricky space because artists deserve to be paid. And we live in a capitalist society and so the way that we assign value is through capital. And professional artists need to be paid wages to show the value of their professional art.

Who are the artistic directors who have most inspired you?

As a young artist the work that Bill Rauch did at Cornerstone was very important to me. He would identify an urgent question within a community and then make a piece with that community about that question. And he would bring in professional artists to work alongside them. So a professional playwright might take their question and put it into a theatrical form and professional actors would act alongside them. And then he would produce that work in a space that the community would go to. So if he was doing a piece about migrant workers, it might end up being performed on a migrant farm.

Then there is the work of Jack Reuler at Mixed Blood. His vision is based on the idea that there is culturally specific storytelling but also that race is construct. And so he produces work that asks questions from many different cultural viewpoints throughout a season, but what you see on the stage looks like a mixed world. He has recently developed a concept of radical hospitality by asking: 'How can we ensure that anyone has access to this space?' And he's got so many initiatives under that umbrella. One of which is that if you buy a ticket for a show, then you can come back to see it again as many times as you like for free, so long as there's space. So you might bring someone back with you. Or you might just come back to be more deeply engaged with what the artist is doing. And then after each show, there's an audience conversation – not a talk back. It is not about artists sitting on the stage and talking from on high, or the audience critiquing the work to the artist. Rather, a member of staff comes out and facilitates the audience to have a conversation among themselves. The theatre is situated right next door to public housing. And there is someone who lives in that housing that is a member of staff, and they are a direct conduit between the residents and the theatre.

Oskar Eustis is also very important to me. He is a phenomenal dramaturge and artistic director. He can think in different forms and he helps artists get closer to their vision by really being in the muck of it with them. Also, George Wolfe and Bill T. Jones are both very important to me. As a young black man, my anger was something that I hid because I was afraid that it, combined with my blackness, would create a volatile situation in which society wouldn't accept me. But watching the way that they use their anger and their disgust at the world around them to propel them to make great and necessary art was really inspiring.

18
KULLY THIARAI

Kully Thiarai ran the Leeds-based touring company Red Ladder Theatre from 1994 to 1998. She then reinvented Contact Theatre in Manchester with a new artistic vision and operational model as a space dedicated to young people. She was then artistic director of the Leicester Haymarket Theatre and founding artistic director of Cast in Doncaster, which opened in 2013. In 2016 she took over National Theatre of Wales – an English-language non-building-based company.

Can you tell me about your journey through the many organizations that you've run?

I come from a working-class family where culture and theatre didn't figure very much. I think I'd been taken to a few shows when I was at school, but other than that I had no sense of theatre having anything to do with me. I went to a school where nothing was expected of anybody – we were all factory fodder. I remember my maths teacher telling me I only needed to learn this stuff so that I would know how to count my husband's money! That was the mindset of a lot of adults around us and it's why I initially ended up wanting to be a social worker. I'd meet youth workers or social workers, and quite often it felt like they were failing us and our communities. And I felt that if I didn't approve of how things were, then I should try and do something about it. So I went to Bradford University to study social work.

It was there that I discovered Theatre in the Mill – which was part of the university. And I started seeing groups like Gay Sweatshop and Phoenix Dance and others. I joined the drama group and ended up working with Ruth Mackenzie who had just started there as a Fellow in Theatre. And she created a piece of work based on transcripts of the trial of the Bradford Twelve, which was quite a big political issue at the time. It was part devised, part written by her, and she directed it. And we took it into youth clubs and so on. That was my first taste of performing.

Then, in my final year, I got this phone call from someone saying I'd been recommended by Ruth to help out with a theatre company called Red Ladder. They had just gone through a big crisis and had appointed a new artistic director, and she wanted to take the company back to its roots by focusing on young people. As a trainee social worker, you have to go and work in the field as part of your degree. And I'd been practising in Bradford, working with the youth service and so I had a lot of traction with young people.

So they enticed me to come along and spend some time with them. That was the first time I began to realize that there could be an activist-type of theatre that was issue based and trying to create conversations. I did an initial six weeks work for them, looking at the key strategic relationships they had in Bradford, Sheffield and Leeds in terms of their community engagement. Once I'd finished that work I ended up being persuaded to be a sort of stage manager or company manager, even though I knew nothing about stage management. I toured with them for a couple years, and it was great because I was sitting in rehearsal rooms watching directors, writers and actors work. I learned a lot through that process.

After about two-and-a-half years with Red Ladder, I said: 'Look guys, I trained as a social worker. I should go and do that really.' So that's what I did. I went and worked in places like the Buttershaw estate, where *Rita, Sue and Bob Too* was set – Andrea Dunbar's world. It was very frontline with a lot of child abuse cases and so on. I was doing long-term family work. When I had first started out, our work was about doing preventative engagement with families. But by this point, in the late 1980s, Thatcher had been in power for about ten years, and it became much more about policing so that was when I decided I had to leave. I remember I was involved in a very big child abuse case, and we had to go and do this dawn raid, with the police, and pull all these kids out. I was very fortunate in that I had a great senior team and real support, and we were able to do a load of therapeutic work with those kids in a very safe space. But that sort of support was being taken away on a daily basis. Yet in some of my direct work with young people, I was using lots of drama techniques that I'd learned – drama games and things to get people to open up. So I was beginning to realize that there might be other ways in which I could still have an impact on those communities and those young people who were at risk.

At the same time, a lot of people were saying to me: 'I think you should be a director.' Of course, in the 1980s, Asian or black artists were predominantly based in London and were either working with Tara Arts or Talawa Theatre Company or The Black Theatre Co-operative. So the assumption was that your job would be at Tara – or one of those companies – and that's where you belonged. I remember there was me and an actress who was from the north-west, and people used to confuse us for being the same person – because there obviously couldn't be more than one person up north who was an Asian woman! I ended up working for Major Road – a national touring company based in Yorkshire. So I spent a year or so with them on a full-time basis as their trainee director working on a number of projects and some of their major touring shows.

After that, I'd been working as a freelancer for a little while when the Red Ladder artistic director job came up. And I didn't think I'd get it, but again, a lot of people were incredibly supportive and said I should apply. This was in the early 1990s when to call yourself a socialist, feminist theatre company was problematic. Rumour had it that the government wanted to get rid of any company with the word 'red' in its name! I did about four years at Red Ladder where I gave people like Roy Williams their first commission. We toured his play *Josie's Boys* around youth clubs.

We also set up the Asian Theatre School. That started as a collaboration between myself at Red Ladder and Kate Chapman at Theatre in the Mill. We always had a policy of having an integrated company, and it became clear that trying to find young Asian actors from Yorkshire was really hard – there was very little opportunity for them. So we set up this summer school, and Kate and I started making work with them, and a few of them then went on to become professional. That became a model that the Arts Council got very excited about and so the Asian Theatre School became an adjunct of Red Ladder for several years before it then spun out as an independent company called Freedom Studios.

And then you took over Contact Theatre in Manchester?

Contact had this £5 million capital development project that had been going on for a long time. The company had lost its way a bit – they'd lost a lot of staff, they'd had a fire, there were delays and so on. The board wanted someone to initially come in on an interim basis and reimagine what it could be. So we developed a three-year plan – we had the first year's programme worked out in order to get the opening sorted, and we then recruited for an artistic director – because I was going to have a baby – which is when John E. McGrath came on board. I then took over from John at National Theatre of Wales (NTW) so he and I have always had this very close connection.

In the meantime I'd also gone down to Leicester Haymarket, which was where I spent nearly seven years as co-artistic director. That was a completely different beast. It was one of the big regional players and I got to make work that was on a very different scale. So I've had these moments where I've done big jobs that have been full-time leadership roles and then periods where I've stopped and been a freelance director and done a lot of strategic consultancy work. I was involved in facilitating some of the creative discussions around the merging of the Library Theatre and Cornerhouse in Manchester to become the new venue: Home. And I was involved in the McMaster report: *Supporting Excellence in the Arts*.

Do you think it was that capacity for strategic thought that drew you to the complex beast that was Cast in Doncaster?

Well, I think when I took the job at Cast, people just thought I was mad! There had been so much controversy around this new building and resistance to it from the local community. But at the interview they asked a really fascinating question. It was: 'What's your vision for the arts in Doncaster?' And this was interesting because it wasn't 'What's your vision for the arts at Cast?' Rather, they specifically asked about Doncaster. And to this day, I don't know whether they realized the subtlety of that question. It might have been quite accidental or it might have been that they had thought about it. But it was a very astute question because it really made me think: 'Why this building, in this place? What is it for?' I guess, ultimately, that is the reason why I said yes to the job. I could see that this iconic building was, despite all the negativity around it in terms of the community and the council, actually an extraordinary investment for a town. And that could fundamentally shift something in the cultural landscape.

We had to be really imaginative because we didn't have much money. It wasn't like we were a producing theatre and could therefore put on loads of shows. We had to be dynamic and smart about partnership working and collaborating. We had to find other sources of money and make the case for doing things differently. For me this didn't feel that hard because I'd done that kind of thing in lots of different places.

One of the good things about people not focusing on you, for whatever reason, is that you just get on and do stuff. If I had done in London some of the things I did in Leicester or Manchester, the response would have been very different. The Cast story is really interesting because when we opened in that September, we couldn't get the *Guardian* or anybody to take any notice. But by January they were chasing us for a feature because it became clear that something was really happening. We got this big half-page spread in the news section about how something extraordinary was happening with this venue and how many people were coming. And having a good new story in a major paper made a really big difference in the town.

But to go back to your question about what drew me to Cast, if I unpick it all, it's about my fundamental value system. I grew up in a context where I didn't have many opportunities or very much access to the arts at all. So I recognize what it feels like not to have that kind of voice. And I also recognize what happens when you give a community or a bunch of artists the voice to say something. It can be hugely powerful for an audience that doesn't often see themselves reflected in that way.

And now you're at the National Theatre of Wales. Everything you've said makes it obvious why you're such a good match for a company that's put so much emphasis on combining community work with professional work.

It's interesting when people ask me: 'Was your career planned?' I say: 'No'. It's just that things seem to have come together this way. It didn't occur to me to apply for the National Theatre of Wales job because I just thought it had been such a huge success and so there would be brilliant Welsh artists who were more suited to it. It wasn't until I was rung up and asked if I would consider it, that it even occurred to me really.

But NTW is an extraordinary company, and there is a value system attached to that notion of having a bespoke model for each show and for the engagement you do, which is really exciting. But I'm trying to forget that it's a national company because that freaks me out a bit! In a job like this, often your personal profile is important. But I've always been about just getting on and doing things relatively quietly as opposed to shouting about it. I always think my role is about facilitating and holding the ground for other people to make the best work.

You are fairly early on in your time here, but how will you go about programming seasons of work?

I'm constantly thinking: 'How do we remain a radical and relevant company?' With each project you have to ask: 'What does this mean for us at this moment? What does it mean for our artists, for our communities?' In general, I absolutely want to honour the legacy and the value systems on which the company is founded. Our focus has always been on making work about communities and place. So in terms of the work for this year and next, it is, when you unpick it, all about asking: 'How do we empower people to have a voice?' We have to understand that ideas can come from anywhere. And now more than ever we need to be thinking about the different ways that we can honour our relationship to each other and be more responsive to our collective humanity.

So there are a disparate number of ways that we develop work. We try to enable artists to explore their thinking without pressure and see what emerges from that. Sometimes that can take a long time and sometimes that might happen very quickly. But also, I'll think: 'Well, what do we really need to be talking about?' And then I'll think about which artist we might want to approach to have that conversation. One of the wonderful things about the company is that everybody has it in their DNA. It feels like we all get why we're here and why we want to do what we want to do. So I don't feel like I've got to be this strident artistic director who has to come up with all the ideas – because there is a massive resource and opportunity that is already there.

Does it ever feel problematic to you that you are not Welsh? Or does being an outsider help?

I do feel conscious that I am living in a different nation from England. And every now and again that hits home. But what's fascinating for me is that, in a way, I'm an outsider in England and an outsider in Wales. Even in recent years I could walk in to a room and be the only woman there, or the only Asian woman there. And in a funny sort of way I think there's an element of the Welsh who see the English as being 'something else' but who, in a way, see me as not being English – so maybe I get a pass because I'm a bit different!

One word that crops up in conversation a lot in the arts world at the moment is 'diversity'. What does that term mean to you?
Whether we like it or not, the story of the theatre industry over the last thirty years has been that whenever there have been cuts, we've lost a lot of BME artists and companies because that's where the cuts have fallen most heavily. People talk a lot about diversity and inclusivity, but actually, for much of the time, these are just great words followed by very little action. I've sat in lots of rooms where people are saying: 'I'm really passionate about diversity.' And I feel like saying to them: 'Well, you can absolutely do something about it. You don't need more money. You're just choosing not to.' Now that might be down to conscious or unconscious biases about gender or race or class playing themselves out. But we know that if you want to put your mind to it, you can overcome these. Years ago people would say: 'Well, there's no talent out there.' I've sat in rooms where senior artistic directors have said to me: 'I don't know any black directors who can direct on our main stage,' and I just think: 'I can't believe you just said that to me.' You can't even argue that one anymore because there's a wealth and breadth of extraordinary talent.

To give you specific example of how we put diversity at the heart of our work – at the moment we're developing a new work in collaboration with an Indian company as part of the British Council Wales' India year. We're working with people who are from that diaspora – who have got very strong Welsh roots and have also got Indian heritage. And many of the women whom we've met through that have told us that they've never had this kind of opportunity before – they've never been able to find out more about their own stories. They are part of a very invisible community in Wales.

We touched on Brexit earlier, and obviously Trump is looming large for all of us at the moment. What role do you think theatre has in relation to the current political climate?
I think there is an interesting distinction between what role *does* it play and what role *should* it play. Sometimes the theatre community talks

as if it's really politically active but actually we're not really, not by any stretch of the imagination. Occasionally we might do a play or a series of plays that might tackle a subject head on, but often that doesn't really connect with lots of communities. The majority of our theatres don't reach the audiences that they really need to reach.

We have to fight for culture as an everyday right. And that isn't about protecting our own little pot of money; it's about being active citizens. It's about shouting about the need for arts to be in schools and for every kid to have an experience of cultural activity. We have to fight to encourage curiosity and playfulness and a sense of the power that imagination can give you. The demise of arts in schools can be a really powerful tool to stop people understanding that they've got some agency over their lives and to stop them imagining a different type of being. But I don't think the artistic community has done very much to galvanize around that. And when we do come out about things, we're in danger of being seen as this whinging, artistic clique that's only out for ourselves.

I suspect that there are a lot of artists who are not part of the mainstream who would agree that that's how we come across. So the greatest thing we can do is to really understand where we sit in the wider ecology. Also, if we have a venue we have to really think about what that means to our community and how do we really, genuinely connect with it. I'm really fascinated with what's happening with pricing at the moment.

Who are the artistic directors who've inspired you in your life?
I always thought that what Jude Kelly was doing at the West Yorkshire Playhouse was really interesting – moving into that new building and galvanizing people around that. I think her passion and intent was always solid. And, of course, I think John E. McGrath has always been brilliant. He made Contact in Manchester into something quite extraordinary. And the passion, intent and values that he brought to National Theatre Wales have been profound and have had a massive impact. I always found Libby Mason fascinating – she ran Theatre Centre in London, a very long time ago. She had a passion for new work and new writing and did a huge amount of pioneering work for young people. She was always incredibly charismatic and really open to new ways of doing things. But she was also fierce in a good way. And Alicia Talbot turned Urban Theatre Projects in Sydney, Australia, into a really dynamic company.

Then, in terms of my own peers, when Rupert Goold was at Northampton and I was at Leicester, we had a really interesting ongoing conversation and a shared sense of purpose about what we were trying to do. And, of course, David Lan did an extraordinary job at the Young Vic. It's really interesting to see how somebody who is in one place for such a long period of time can take it from being one thing and really slowly augment it until it is something quite different.

19
ERICA WHYMAN

Erica Whyman was artistic director of the unfunded fringe theatre Southwark Playhouse from 1999 to 2001. She then took over at the Gate Theatre from 2001 to 2004 where she oversaw its inclusion in the Arts Council's portfolio of core-funded organizations. She ran Northern Stage in Newcastle from 2005 to 2012, a major regional theatre that has a main space which seats 450 and two smaller studio spaces. Since 2013 she has been deputy artistic director of the Royal Shakespeare Company.

Can you start by telling me about your journey through the various artistic directorships you've had?
I always knew that I wanted to run a building. I remember doing the young director's course at the National Theatre, and Peter Hall asked: 'Who here wants to be an artistic director?' I stuck my hand up assuming that at least half of us would also do so, but it was just me. That stayed with me – I had always assumed that everybody would want to. Why the hell wouldn't you? But the majority of directors don't.

Within six months of that, I was running Southwark Playhouse. I was young and I was terrified of the responsibility of it. But I think the impulse to do it came from having an interest in the *whole* experience of the audience. I'm not interested in just making the art. I am also interested in lots of different processes. I really like questions like: 'How do you make a team function in such a way that it's happy and motivated and can do the best work?' Accountability is also a big thing for me. It doesn't sit easily with me the idea that you are entitled to be an artist or that, if you are lucky enough to be an artist, you don't have to worry about how that is afforded or why society is enabling you to do it.

The thread that goes all the way through to now is the sense that a good rehearsal room is a really interesting model of how to organize authority. What's changed is that I've got more and more confident that if you get the right kind of rehearsal room, you can use it as a model for many, many other kinds of team work. It becomes the same thing as other forms of leadership. It's not a separate idea suitable only for making theatre.

So Southwark was this tiny place and none of us had any cash. There were three of us running the theatre and we were all effectively working full-time for less than part-time wages. We were working dawn until dusk: tearing tickets, running the bar, dealing with the rat infestation and so on. It was a sort of mad, romantic time but completely brilliant. We had no Arts Council funding, and we only had a little bit from Southwark Council for our education work. So the learning curve was huge and I quickly learned a few things about my principles. For instance when I started, we didn't pay actors but we did by the end.

The key turning point at Southwark was when I directed a production of *The Winter's Tale* that involved the most chutzpah that I had shown to date. The Globe was in the process of opening that summer and I thought: 'We're going to offer a different kind of Shakespeare' – which shows a fantastic kind of ego really! We did it with an amazing company of nine actors and I paid them £100 a week and I spent quite a lot of money on PR and so on. Opening night was a real turning point for me because we filled the building with the great and the good, and suddenly people were watching what we were up to. It was a very exciting night, we did a brilliant show, but there were no press there at all – and I knew there were no press. So I had this horrible feeling that I had persuaded so many people that this can work, but I hadn't delivered the key thing that was going to fill the theatre for the next four weeks – reviews.

The next day I was on a coach going somewhere, and Lucy Briers, who was playing Paulina, rang me and said: 'Look, we've got nine people in the audience. What do we do?' And I said that: 'Our deal was that we needed to have more people in the audience than in the cast, so if you chose not to do it tonight I would respect that.' But she said: 'Okay. We're doing it.' And it turned out that *Time Out* were in that night. And they gave it a terrific review, but they didn't put it in Critics' Choice. And a week or so later, a colleague said to me: 'Why don't you ring them up and tell them that they should have put it in Critics' Choice?' And so I did and then they did and we sold out. It was that simple – on the back of one review. This is all led me to understand the kind of levers you have to pull sometimes. That story matters to me because it makes it clear that it can be all very well running your team and making good work, but if you can't pull the levers that can change the narrative about the theatre you're running, then you might as well not be doing it.

And so then you went on to run the Gate. And you made massive changes there – it was under you that the theatre received core funding from the Arts Council for the first time.

Yes. And that required a whole other form of leadership. It was incredibly difficult and I learned an enormous amount about change. In theory that was a hugely positive moment for the Gate. But it was hard because what I learned is that there are always losses when things change. In this case, we lost what my predecessor Mick Gordon would call 'the passion machine'. By which he meant that the thing that is precious about the Gate is that everyone's doing it for nothing. And I am actually incredibly grateful for his challenge. Because it helped me to very sharply describe my leadership from then on. I'd say: 'That's not okay because who can afford to do that? It's not serving the industry. It's not living our principles, so it's not alright.'

The other way it was formative was that I came up against myself at the Gate in a way that I didn't at Southwark Playhouse. I've always had a very keen sense of social justice and a belief that theatre is a way of talking about what's wrong in our world. I applied to the Gate because it seemed to me an extraordinary place to do that, given the international lens the theatre had. My first season had a show about terrorism and a show about the abolition of slavery at a point when we were reconsidering race relations in London. But famously Jane Edwardes in *Time Out* said: 'Oh, it feels a bit A level to me.' By which she meant: 'None of this is glittery. Where are the celebrities? These don't feel like thrilling nights out.' That was so demoralizing!

I always felt the Gate was a place to take risks. And that required a seriousness of purpose in terms of the ideas we were tackling. But I got an enormous amount of feedback going: 'We just want a brilliant night out.' But actually, 9/11 happened while I was teaching a show at the Gate, and then, of course, there was the financial crash. So those things have created a real sense for me that the seriousness of theatre is something we all need and want. But that was completely absent in the early 2000s.

The culture I was working in felt like it was resisting what I thought was going to happen which was that we were going to need to talk about the state of the world – that something was crumbling. And actually the minute I resigned, there were suddenly all these articles going: 'Oh my God, the Gate had this wonderful integrity and clarity of purpose.' And I think that was because the world had started to turn by the time I left. Personally, it was an incredibly difficult time. It was really hard – feeling so deeply unfashionable.

And did you get pressure from your board?

Yes, there was huge pressure from the board. People were asking: 'Why can't we have two hits in a row?' But I remember the brilliant Jonathan Hull, who worked in the commercial theatre, said in that board meeting: 'If the Gate starts to think it needs two hits in a row, we're sunk. Because even those of us who are trying to have hits know we can't get two hits in a row. So if the Gate isn't allowed to fail how can any of us learn?' The sense that that's not what we're for – we're for something else – was very helpful. And I had a huge wave of support from artists. There was this great body of people who were making sacrifices to be part of the work. I remember there was this sort of *West Wing*[1] 'let Bartlett be Bartlett' moment, where I wobbled on a season, and the team went: 'No, we should do it anyway, despite everything.'

That's something I've always found really exciting about running a building – when you have a team that will hold you to account by your own standards. I think that's a sign that you've actually managed to inculcate in that team a real sense of mission and purpose.

I completely agree. It's an amazing moment when they say: 'Oh no, we see the risk that you are running and we will be the ones to carry the results of that risk. It will be harder for us to raise money. It will be harder for us to put bums in seats. But we don't get ourselves out of

[1]American political drama created by Aaron Sorkin that ran from 1999 to 2006.

this by going backwards. We get ourselves out of this by going forward with the mission and sticking true to our guns.' And, of course, at the Gate, it's maddening if you only have thirty-five people in a 70-seat theatre. But there's not much difference financially between thirty-five and seventy. And if you're getting it right with those thirty-five, then stick to your guns and the rest will come. That was a huge lesson about holding my nerve.

Then you went to Northern Stage. Why did you want to run another building given that the Gate had been so difficult? And how different is it running a small theatre in London compared to a big theatre that's not in London?

The answer to the first question is that I declared to the board of the newly inaugurated Clore Leadership Programme that I didn't want to run another building. And luckily, they went: 'Sure, we hear you but let's see what happens.' And they gave me a fellowship for which I'm genuinely eternally grateful. I was feeling quite bruised and quite confused because I knew I still wanted to lead or I wouldn't have applied for the fellowship, but I didn't know what. And they really heard what that dilemma was and tapped into my sense that what I truly wanted to do was change the world. And theatre is evidently completely inadequate as tool with which to do that, but it's also really compelling – it's really specific in the thing that it can do. Chris Smith, the then director of the programme, was particularly helpful. I was thinking that maybe I wanted to go back to being a philosopher. But he looked me in the eye and said: 'I don't think you want a contemplative life. You want periods of contemplation and you want periods to think about these ideas because ideas excite you. But I think you want to get your sleeves rolled up and make things happen.' And he was quite right about that.

When the job at Northern Stage came up, it was at a very odd moment in the theatre's history. They were in the middle of building work that had got behind, and the then executive director and artistic director weren't talking to each other. The organization was divided down the middle and was miserable. It had lost its audience. So the board basically decided that artistic directors were not to be trusted and advertised for a chief executive. If they had not made that decision I would never have applied – because it got my blood up! They put out a four-page job description, and on page four it said: 'Some experience in the arts would be an advantage.' Scandalous! So I applied feeling like I didn't have very much to lose as I wasn't going to get the job. They pushed me very hard on whether I'd have applied if it had been advertised as artistic director and executive director separately. In all conscience I said: 'Actually that structure doesn't interest me if it suggests that the artistic director is not accountable and not responsible for raising the money and having a reasonable business model and so on.' So we agreed that I would be chief executive and artistic director and I'd then have an administrative director. I found that to be a tremendous liberation because that model didn't exist before.

There were many things that were incredibly difficult. We were building an audience from nothing – once we really got the stats, we saw that there were only 200 people coming regularly. I had a new building that was going to cost more than twice as much as the old one. It was very frightening. I remember looking at these endless diagrams trying to make the model work and avoid any kind of deficit. Of course I put this huge pressure on myself so there would not be a crack in my ability to lead the business.

It was also hard having a team of about forty-five people who were initially very unhappy. It took about two years to persuade them around. But then, it was like converts to anything; they were incredibly supportive once they came on board. I worked harder than I'd ever worked anywhere on developing that team. We did crazy things – we did a citywide treasure hunt as our company outing so that they could learn about the insides of every other cultural organization. I made nine of the cultural organizations in the city set us treasure hunt tasks. It was completely bonkers but absolutely memorable. The task I set myself was 'Take them with you.' Their love of the city and their love of the building were immense, but they had been really let down by some difficult times. By 2012 they were so motivated and courageous that we opened a venue in Edinburgh running eleven shows a day.

So now you're the deputy artistic director at the RSC – a national company but based in a tiny place: Stratford-upon-Avon. How does that differ from previous jobs?

It's the national remit of the RSC that really interests me. And the best example of that has been doing our recent production of *A Midsummer Night's Dream* where we brought together professional actors with amateur companies to play the mechanicals and local children as the fairies. It's genuinely the most transformative thing I've ever done. People who thought they wouldn't enjoy it, or wouldn't have access to it, or would be excluded from it, came because their friends and most critically their children were in it. It was the parents' response that was most moving. They were often deeply sceptical initially – the fact that their children were in an RSC production meant nothing to them. This is because all the schools we worked with were in places that had very low cultural opportunity. So everywhere we went, we had parents going: 'This doesn't mean anything to me. I've got more important things to do like putting a roof over their head.' But then they would be changed by seeing their kids do it – seeing their kids rise to a challenge in front of an audience and speak those words and know what they meant and have access to a central part of English culture or British culture, which will change their fortunes. I saw parents saying: 'I had no idea that was what they could do and now I will have higher expectations of them in every sense.'

Most importantly I just saw people really thrilled that they're included. I'd seen a devastating and consistent absence of confidence, even in people who were not on the poverty line. I saw it in people who are nurses and pub landlords and funeral directors. People who in their working lives felt that no one cared about them and no one trusted them. So to find that their voice was valued was astonishing to them. That they were considered to be equals with us in the process of making the work, that a national organization valued and trusted them, was very marked and very moving. This was consistent across eighty-four amateur actors from fourteen different groups in twelve different places.

It's here that Shakespeare becomes really useful. He's just a brilliant lever because he isn't going away, he's ours and he's our country's culture. He challenges you, through the mechanicals, at the end of *Dream,* to say: 'Actually I'd rather see the guys who have tried and failed than see the most polished production of that ancient Roman tale.' Isn't that an amazing and beautiful thing? And he values real work in that play and in many plays. He shows that being a carpenter or a weaver is an honourable thing to do. He recognizes that that is what most people do – most people are not kings and queens or dukes and duchesses, or indeed actors. So Shakespeare feels like this extraordinary tool for giving people a sense that they do belong in our culture and that culture is relevant to them.

One of the big things dominating our industry at the moment is the discussion around diversity. How do you see your role in relation to that conversation?

Well, I now believe that we need consistent, positive action on all fronts. And that is a change for me. I grew up as a director in places like Southwark and Notting Hill that, both in terms of ethnic background and social background, were places of tremendous and vivid diversity. And I did think it was going to change by osmosis. I thought: 'We all know this, and we all know that the range of artists we work with needs to be more diverse and more actively representative of the groups that aren't represented. That's going to happen because my generation gets it.' But I see very clearly now that that did not work. We allowed certain kinds of representation to become very siloed. We became very excited about black-led companies or Asian-led companies and that's important, but it doesn't change whatever we want to think of as the mainstream.

And, of course, class has come up the agenda for me. I think nationally it has come up the agenda. You can't expect these things to change if your criterion for entering and surviving the profession is that you already have to have some kind of financial security. And we, as an industry, can be terrible snobs. We claim that we're interested in class and that we want to commission and produce plays about class. But we don't actually want to employ someone whose career has mainly been in Stockton, Blackpool, Taunton or Margate. Somehow we have this idea that there's a peripheral ring where the work can't be good because it is not happening where we are. That's just got to stop. We have to go and see it and judge it on its merits. Some of that we can blame on critics. But actually, if we know they aren't seeing the work, then we have to go and see the work. It's just not true that by default the work isn't good enough unless it's made it to London.

To come back to artistic directorship more generally, sometimes you have to make quite tough choices. And that can mean saying 'no' to the brilliant white man in the room, for example, and even some of the brilliant white women. We might say: 'That's a great project. But for countless generations those projects have found a route to the stage. They have always been funded and supported, so now we have to fund and support something else if we're going to make a different mix.' And that might make things much harder for some of those white men and some of those white women. But it's time to move over and make space. The decision not to diversify is a decision to continue to make work by a certain kind of person, whether that's defined by their educational background, the colour of their skin or their gender.

I also think that very early interventions are important, around directors in particular. We need to see more directors of colour in those gatekeeper roles. I famously said last year we don't need more female artistic directors. We need more feminists. But what I meant is we don't *only* need more female artistic directors, but we need more feminists. And, of course, the same is true across all aspects of diversity.

Who are the artistic directors who have inspired you in your life?

Richard Eyre – he was my Clore mentor. When I was at university and afterwards, I grew up with his programme at the National. What I loved about it was the intertwining of really rigorous, complex, intriguing ideas with a massive heart. He was incredibly helpful as a mentor. When I went to Northern Stage and they wanted to know if I could be truly accountable, he very quietly said to me: 'It's insulting to suggest such an artist can't be accountable and isn't accountable every time they consider making art for an audience.'

Also, Joan Littlewood.[2] I'm not like Joan. She was brutal and difficult and thoroughly uninterested in the establishment, whereas I'm consistently interested in changing the establishment from the inside. But I loved her energy and her ability to knock a wall down with the work. And she cared about audiences in a real sense.

And, of course, Buzz Goodbody.[3] I'm not like her either. And she was much younger than me, of course, when she was here. But what inspires me is that theatre was political for her, through and through, like a stick of rock. She was sure that Shakespeare had something to

---

[2]Artistic director and founder of Theatre Workshop which was the resident company at Theatre Royal Stratford East where she was artistic director from 1953 to 1974.

[3]The first woman to direct at the RSC. She played a key role in establishing The Other Place in 1974 – the RSC's first studio theatre in Stratford-upon-Avon. She passed away in 1975.

say about that and that this place, the RSC, was redeemable – could really reach people. Obviously, I'm not interested in closing our national institutions down and doing without them. But I do think they need to be accurately and rigorously critiqued from the inside and the outside. And she did that very well.

20
MADANI YOUNIS

Madani Younis was founding artistic director of Freedom Studios in Bradford which he ran until 2011 when he took over as artistic director at the Bush Theatre in Shepherd's Bush, London. The Bush is a flexible studio space that seats between 160 and 200 and champions new plays and new writers. In September 2018 (after this interview was conducted), it was announced that he had been appointed as the next creative director of the Southbank Centre in London.

Could you tell me about your journey to becoming artistic director of the Bush?

I graduated from Birmingham University having done an MPhil in playwriting studies under David Edgar. I then returned to London, having been born here, and did that thing of writing letters to all the major buildings and companies asking for work. But I was met by a wall of silence. Ultimately, I wanted to write and direct my own work. Birmingham had enabled me to work with some amazing playwrights; it was a great form of training, but I wanted the equivalent of that in directing. I couldn't afford to spend another year doing a post-grad in directing. So the route of assistant directing made sense. But that didn't pan out, at least not in London, and that was humbling. I had no familial relationships or connections that I could draw upon to help me get through the door here.

So I went to Trinidad, which is where my mother's family is from. While there, I worked at the Trinidad Theatre Workshop which is the company that Derek Walcott set up. I'd read scripts for them and work with playwrights. Significantly it was the first time I had experienced playwriting through a non-European lens, which was really eye-opening for me. When I was at Birmingham, your understanding of playwriting begins with Aristotle's poetics and then you learn all these rules. For example, you are told that using flashback is a clunky expositional device that is frowned upon and demonstrates a laziness in the playwright, whereas when you go to Trinidad, you pick up these plays and without exception; they are using flashback. I remember saying to Albert Laveau, who ran the company at the time: 'What's this about?' And he said, 'Well, flashback is used as a storytelling technique that's been born out of a tradition of memory recall. When one contextualizes the idea that these islands are made up of descendants of enslaved Africans, memory recall, as a form of storytelling, allows them to be transported back to a country that they may never have been to before.' That was significant for me because I went: 'Oh, fuck, there are other ways to write these things that we call plays.' I had learned about everything from the Greeks to the kitchen sink dramas of the post-war period and the plays of the 1970s and 1980s, but there was this other stuff too. That was an important moment for me.

Then, in the early 2000s, an opportunity arose to work at Red Ladder Theatre Company (RLTC). They wanted to appoint a director of the Asian Theatre School, as it was known then. That was a summer school project that had been started, essentially, to address the imbalance of second- and third-generation South Asian performers coming into the profession. So I moved to Leeds where RLTC were based and I just started making work with the communities of Bradford. I'd always been inspired by artists like Spike Lee, Shane Meadows, Mike Leigh, Woody Allen, Horace Ove – people who made work about their own communities. I loved the idea of localism and of using both professional and non-professional performers. So I was working with people of all ages and we started making these really big epic pieces. And we won some awards and we started touring. And a number of people said to me: 'You should set up a company. You could separate from Red Ladder and do your own thing.' I remember the Arts Council saying: 'Look, you could argue a case and we'd be receptive to listening to it.' So we did, and thus was born Freedom Studios in Bradford.

That journey, in my twenties, to becoming artistic director of my own company also allowed me to understand what it meant to fundraise, to operate a lighting desk, to sew costumes, to market a show and so on. That 'grassroots' journey to having a fully-fledged company meant I learned in a very holistic way what it was to be an artistic director. I'd put money on the fact that many artistic directors running buildings today won't have the equivalent skillset that I had when I started my first job!

We never had a building. We started out producing our work in the studios of regional theatres that ranged from about 120 to 320 seats. But eventually we decided to make work in found spaces. This felt much more political for us because it meant that we could make work in the communities that we were telling the stories of – the communities we actually lived in. We were working in buildings that had scarred the landscape since the textile industry had died in those cities and that felt like a really important political gesture. It also meant we could ensure the money that we were spending on our productions was spent within a mile and a half radius of any site that we were in – we worked with local chippies and electricians. So the public money we were spending wasn't just benefitting us as artists; it actually benefitted the people whose stories we're telling. So we weren't like Christopher Columbus coming in and saying: 'We're here to give you savages culture,' which is how we felt a lot of buildings behaved. To a degree, I still feel that way about how a lot of buildings behave when it comes to immigrant communities into our country.

Making work in these found spaces was amazing. The last show I did, which was called *The Mill: City of Dreams,* cost about £220,000 to make. We gave free tickets for the opening week to people who lived locally and then it was five quid for the lowest priced ticket. But by the last week, it had gone crazy. It sold out and people really wanted to see it and there were very affluent people who paid five hundred quid to see it. Technically they were making a donation, and as part of that donation, they'd be given a ticket. What was beautiful about that was that it meant that people from the most affluent parts of our region were coming to parts of a city that they had only read of or heard of, and as such we were discovering each other in new terms.

So you were bringing people from profoundly different socio-economic backgrounds together in one space?

Totally. And it was during the making of that show that I got a call from Nick Starr, the chair of the Bush Theatre's board at the time, asking if I wanted to apply for the AD job. Initially I was like: 'Look, dude, I'm not sure. I just spent the last three years telling theatre buildings to go fuck themselves. I can't now go and run a building!' But he said: 'Look, at least come for a first interview so we can meet each other.' So I said okay. And I went to that first interview and it was fucking awful. I think it would be fair to say I hated them and they hated me, and I just wanted to get the fuck out of there!

Why was that?
I'd decided that I wasn't going to just go in and name-check London shows or London writers. It's not that I was ignorant and didn't know who they were. But I'd just spent the best part of nine years in Yorkshire. So I thought; 'Im going to come down here and just refer to artists and writers I knew up there. That obviously then creates resistance because they don't know who I'm talking about, and I wasn't willing to talk about the writers that they were more comfortable with. But at least I was being true about what I was bringing to the table. So it just felt like there wasn't any sort of connection. Then, a week later, Nick rings me up and I was expecting him to say: 'We don't want you back.' I'd made my peace with that. But the truth was, I felt like I'd been mugged off. I felt like I was really just there to fill a quota. And he asked me: 'How do you think it went?' And obviously I said it really wasn't a good experience and a lot of expletives followed that! And I'm convinced that, at that moment, Nick had rung to say no to me. Long story short, Nick says: 'Look, we've got to see you again.'

At the second interview, I thought: 'I'm going to be right at the back of the pack of all these people they're seeing.' But that gave me real confidence – it made me think I've got nothing to lose. My only objective at that point was to make them feel my spirit so that they knew who I was as a human being, as an artist and as a leader. I opened with a joke and everyone laughed. And we had an amazing moment together, all of us – it was like we were dancing. It was beautiful. There was no treading on eggshells.

So it was a terrible first date and a good second date?
It was an amazing second date – just real fun. I walked out just thanking God that they'd felt me. I didn't think about it any further. I wasn't even sure that I wanted it. Then, I was in Brazil doing some work for the coalition government and I got a call from Nick saying: 'We'd like to offer it to you.' And I remember asking: 'How long do I have to think about it?' There was a lot to consider: Should I give up a company I started

and that is successful, to move to a building that looks nothing like me to be the first non-white artistic director of a theatre in London ever? I'm not careerist, so I wasn't looking for an opportunity like this. I waited until I got back from Brazil and I went up to Bradford and spoke with some people. A lot of people in the company stopped talking to me when I told them that I was thinking about it. The truth is, when you are an artist of colour who feel like you've been ignored to fuck by buildings like the Bush and many others out there, it's hard to then believe that the opportunity is real and that you're not being played. A lot of people felt like this wasn't a good move for me – that I was just being set up to fail. But ultimately I said yes and the journey began.

It must have been quite a big shift to go from running a company you founded to a building that has such a significant history. Did you feel that history was a burden or something to build on? Did it shape the way you programme? How do you think you managed to reshape theatre?

When you walk into a theatre that has a thirty-eight- or thirty-nine-year history before you arrive, you do look to the past to try and understand where it came from. But with the exception of my predecessor, Josie Rourke, whom I knew before I started here, I don't remember getting a single message from any previous AD of the theatre to say congratulations or to offer advice. That made things very lonely initially. Coupled with that was this London arrogance of feeling like people were thinking: 'Who the fuck is this guy? We've never heard of him before.' Of course, if you were to check the last seven or eight years of the Bush's history prior to me being there, you probably wouldn't have seen a brown director or writer making work on this stage at all. So is it any wonder I suddenly felt like an alien offer to this building? I didn't fit that mould. I'm raised by activists so that shit didn't bother me an ounce, but emotionally it does affect you.

The one thing I learned by looking at the past, and what I still hold onto now, is that the Bush has always been run by mavericks. It's meant to be on the edge and to be an advocate for those on the peripheries: the subversives, the radicals. That's what I got when I look back and I suppose that's who I am. And I felt that the board had bought into my mandate which was quite simply I wanted to make a theatre that belonged to all people, not just some people.

But at the beginning it was awful. I came in and I had twelve weeks to announce the first season. I'm working with commissions that are live but that aren't really mine, I was working with a team that wasn't my own, and there wasn't enough lead in time – but there never is, right? So the first year was as bumpy as fuck. The Bush says it's a new writing theatre and, historically, we've always accepted unsolicited plays come what may. But I just felt like we weren't reading these plays with the intention of actually producing them. We were barely reading them to give notes on them. It just felt like a symbolic gesture. We were somehow obligated to engage with these plays, but we no longer understood why. So I said, pretty clearly, we're only going to read to produce. We will sit down twice a year to plan the next eighteen months, and we will only read during those two windows of time. And I remember a former artistic director coming at me quite publicly and saying: 'No, this is sacrilege!' Yet that same artistic director had never bothered to reach out initially to say congratulations or anything. But I thought: 'If you want to come at me, that's cool.' So the first year was super difficult. I was still finding my rhythm, I was still finding my team and finding myself in this new building and this new part of the city. But in the middle of that first year, when it was really tough, I absolutely knew I was going to deliver in that second year because I knew the work I wanted to make and I knew the artists I wanted to work with. And in that second year we produced some amazing plays; we sold out and we won a number of awards.

How do you go about developing writers? How do you apply what you learned about playwriting in both Birmingham and, by contrast, Trinidad, to finding and developing writers?

When this theatre was first created, there were only two theatres – the Royal Court and us – that were really advocating for new writing. Fast-forward to today and we no longer have a monopoly on new writing. Every theatre across our city has an emerging writer's group, a new play submission policy, etc. We've also seen, in the last fifteen years, the emergence of lots of postgrad, MA or BA playwriting and creative writing courses. As a result, you're seeing the professionalization of writing as a career in real concrete terms.

So the thing that is interesting to me is to ask: 'Where are those people who are writing in ways that don't conform to the solitary idea of sitting behind a desk in a room and just putting pen to paper? Who is rewriting our city in ways that theatre doesn't quite understand yet?' And that leads you to discover people like Michaela Coel, Sabrina Mahfouz, Cush Jumbo and so on. So then you ask: 'What is this building really about? Is it about new writing?' That is a term that no one outside of our industry really understands. Fundamentally, I think we're about telling stories. That's what theatre is about. And the mechanisms for how that story is made can be really varied. So I was always very clear that we were going to commission more widely and spread our risk across a wider sphere of artists. That meant we would still commission writers who wrote in a more familiar or traditional way. So, for example, Vinay Patel will give us a new draft of his play and we'll do a reading of it, or if we feel it needs a workshop, we'll do that. But then, you'll get Arinze Kene, who is a writer and performer developing a solo piece. And we've done endless weeks of R&D on that show – putting it on its feet with musicians, etc. So, now, we're much more bespoke to the idea of the play. We meet the needs of each piece as opposed to trying to transpose a single way of working onto different processes.

What does that word 'community' mean to you? What is the community that the Bush is serving?

I often think that the connotations of the word 'community' make it some sort of fucked-up euphemism for the marginalized or the impoverished or the poor or the destitute or the forgotten. It's as if it is a word to describe any group of people who aren't seen as part of the dominant culture.

But it's really easy for me to define community here at the Bush. My mandate is defined by where we are located: on the Uxbridge Road. It's the longest road in London and the most diverse road in the whole of Europe in terms of the number of languages spoken on it. I believe that the inside of this building should look like the outside of this building and vice versa. How often do we see theatres across the world that are located in quote unquote 'communities' but, in spite of those communities, are making work that has no relation to the place that they are in? I think that is to the detriment of both the arts and to the communities that surround those buildings.

Another word that gets used a lot in our industry at the moment is 'diversity'. You spoke earlier about being the first person of colour to run a London theatre, but obviously there have been some significant further changes in that regard in recent years with Indhu Rubasingham at the Tricycle, Nadia Fall at Theatre Royal Stratford East and Kwame Kwei-Armah at the Young Vic. So what is your perspective on that?

You're absolutely right that in the industry now, the word 'diversity' appears in probably every other conversation I have during my working day, with all kinds of people at all levels of our sector. That certainly wasn't the case when I first started. When I was growing up and there was the inquiry into the murder of Stephen Lawrence, terms like 'institutional racism' entered our national vocabulary and became an immediate reminder that we don't live in a post-racial society. Then, when I started working in the arts, which are often perceived to be left-leaning, bohemian and liberal, I actually discovered that they were conservative, inward-looking and parochial. The thing I believed in still had an entrenched cultural conservatism.

So important steps have been taken when it comes to diversity with, finally, the acknowledgement that something has to change. But the irony for me is we, who are liberal, bohemian and left-leaning, had to have the same level of political pressure exerted upon us before we were willing to look at what we were doing and change it. We weren't leading the pack and saying to everyone else; we know this is fucked up.

At the moment, I feel like we are seeing a corporatization of diversity, which really means we are being asked to barter for our equality with white men and women. But I am no longer prepared to do that. I only need to look back a couple hundred years to understand what happened when my ancestors decided to barter for their equality with white men and women to understand that never works out for us! So I'm not going to subscribe to that because it ultimately becomes about white men and women setting a pace that they are comfortable with. I'm not convinced that an industry that has systematically ignored people of colour is suddenly now best placed to tell people of colour how change should come about. So forgive me if I'm not clapping my hands and writing 'thank you' notes to people!

Who are the artistic directors who have inspired you?
Şermin Langhoff who ran Ballhaus Naunynstraße, in Germany. Her work was fire – she set up a theatre for the Turkish community in Berlin and then went onto run the Gorki. Her focus on servicing her community is, for me, super important. Also, Fred Pinheiro who runs the Nós Do Morro theatre school in Brazil is amazing. You will know what they do because all of the kids in the film *City of God* came from there. So their work is fire too. Another example from Brazil would be José Júnior and his venue AfroReggae – which is an artistic space based in a favela – their work blew my mind too. I'm also a big fan of what Ravi Jain has done at the Why Not Theatre in Toronto, Canada. And in this country, Wendy Harris at Tutti Frutti in Leeds and Michael Buffong at Talawa Theatre are both doing great work.

ABOUT THE AUTHOR

Christopher Haydon was artistic director of the Gate Theatre from 2012 to 2017. Prior to that he was associate director at the Bush Theatre from 2008 to 2011. He was a 2017 fellow of the Clore Leadership Programme. He studied at Cambridge University and trained at the Central School of Speech and Drama, the National Theatre Studio, the Lincoln Center in New York and with Cicely Berry at the RSC.

Directing credits at the Gate include *The Convert, Grounded* (also Traverse Theatre, Studio Theatre Washington, DC, national and international tour; winner: Fringe First, Best Production, Off West End Awards), *Diary of a Madman* (also Traverse Theatre), *The Iphigenia Quartet, The Christians* (also Traverse Theatre; winner: Fringe First), *Image of an Unknown Young Woman* (winner: Best Production, Off West End Awards), *The Edge of Our Bodies, Trojan Women, Purple Heart, The Prophet* and *Wittenburg*.

Freelance directing credits include *Macbeth* (Manchester Royal Exchange), *Remains of the Day* (Northampton Royal and Derngate/Out of Joint), *Trying It On* (China Plate/RSC/Royal Court), *On the Exhale* (China Plate/Traverse Theatre, released as an audiobook by Audible; winner: Fringe First), *The Caretaker* (Bristol Old Vic/Northampton Royal and Derngate), *Twelve Angry Men* (Birmingham Rep/West End), *Sixty-Six Books, In the Beginning* (Bush Theatre/Westminster Abbey), *Grace* and *Pressure Drop* (On Theatre). His first independent short film, *In Wonderland*, was funded by Film London and screened at festivals around the world winning several awards, including Best Drama at the BAFTA-accredited Aesthetica Short Film Festival. His next short film, *Martha*, is being funded by the BFI and will shoot in 2019. Other film credits include *Passages: A Windrush Celebration* (as producer, Royal Court/Black Apron), *Devil in the Detail* (Royal Court/Guardian), *Two*

Gentleman of Verona and *The Taming of the Shrew* (Globe Theatre/ BBC iPlayer).

As a journalist he has written for *The Scotsman, Financial Times*, *Independent*, *Guardian, New Statesman*, *The Stage* and *Prospect Magazine*. Publications include *Conversations on Religion*, *Conversations on Truth* (Continuum) and *Identity and Identification* (Wellcome Collection/Black Dog). He was a contributor to *Adapting Translation for the Stage* (Routledge). His report *Where are the Workers? Class Diversity in British Theatre Audiences* was funded by the AHRC and can be downloaded from the Clore Leadership Programme's website.

He is a trustee of Theatre Peckham and a selector for the National Student Drama Festival. His Twitter handle is @chrishaydon99.